A Moose and a Lobster Walk into a Bar . . .

Also from Islandport Press

Father Fell Down the Well by Kendall Morse

Down the Road a Piece by John McDonald

Live Free and Eat Pie by Rebecca Rule

Finding Your Inner Moose by Susan Poulin

Thoughts of an Average Joe by Brian Daniels

A Moose and a
Lobster Walk
into a Bar . . .

John McDonald

ISLANDPORT PRESS

ISLANDPORT PRESS

PO Box 10
247 Portland Street
Yarmouth, ME 04096
www.islandportpress.com
info@islandportpress.com

ISBN: 978-1-944762-37-7
Library of Congress Control Number: 2002109648

First edition published August 2002
Fifteenth anniversary edition published November 2017.

Book design by Islandport Press
Cover photography by Jill Brady

To Ann, with love

Acknowledgments

I am grateful to the many newspaper editors who one by one made the decision to publish my stories. My thanks go especially to Tom Kelch, former executive editor of the *Lewiston Sun Journal,* who first suggested I write a weekly column and then agreed to carry it in his newspaper.

I am also grateful to my editor and publisher, Dean Lunt of Islandport Press, who said he saw a book in these writings and was determined to find it.

This book and many others would not be possible without public libraries and the helpful people who staff them. I particularly want to thank Mike Dignan of the South Paris Public Library and Ann Siekman at the Norway Library.

Thanks must also go to my storytelling friend and colleague, Kendall Morse, the Down East storyteller most of us think of when we think of Down East stories. And a thank you should probably go to my other colleagues in the storytelling community. They know who they are and what they've done.

There are so many other people I should thank at this point—like all those folks through the years who have contributed to our store of Down East stories. Because I can't possibly name them all, I will just acknowledge their important contributions.

And, most important, I would like to thank my wife Ann for her unflagging support and encouragement during the seven long and sometimes difficult years that this book was "under construction."

John McDonald
South Paris, Maine

Contents

Fifteen Years!

My idea was to start writing a weekly column of about a thousand words and see if I could get a few weekly papers to print it. Tom Kelch, former executive editor of the *Lewiston Sun Journal*, was the first to agree to carry my column in his newspaper, and my first column appeared in the *Sun Journal* on June 1, 1995. By summer's end my column was in eight weekly newspapers. My plan, I thought, was off to a good start.

When I had written over one hundred columns I began thinking it might be time to start shopping them around to publishers. As host of a weekend talk show on WGAN radio, I often have authors on as guests to talk about their recently published books. After interviewing Maine historian William Lemke, on his latest book, I asked if he would mind giving me contact information for his publisher in Massachusetts. He said "sure" and wrote out all the information I needed. The contact lead to a book, but not a book featuring my columns. That would have to wait, but I didn't abandon the idea.

Then one day there was an article in the Portland Press Herald about Dean Lunt, who had just started Islandport Press in Yarmouth. Looking through the phone book (remember phone books?) I got his number and called him. He said he knew of me and had even read my column in *The Notes*, a local weekly based in Yarmouth. He asked if there was a place online where he could read the columns and I sent him a link. A few days later we agreed to meet for lunch to discuss "the book." Eventually Dean sent me a contract.

I can't remember how long it took—and it's not important now—but one fine day I received a package from Islandport that contained the galley proofs of what would become *A Moose and a Lobster Walk into a Bar*. My wife and

I divided the proofs in half and spent the afternoon reading the book. Afterwards we agreed that Dean had done a good job dividing the columns into themes and editing the manuscript. We were pleased.

Then, all we could do is wait for the book to be printed, bound, and shipped back to Islandport in Yarmouth. I can't remember the circumstances, but I happened to be at Dean's place soon after the first 3,500 books arrived. It was good to see. That was the first edition, and the more than one hundred boxes just about filled Dean's garage.

Then came the radio, TV and newspaper interviews, to let readers and others know that my columns were now a book and now available at fine bookstores throughout northern New England. (I would add that if a bookstore didn't have copies of my book on its shelves, then it just wasn't a fine bookstore.) So, my modest goal of having a book of columns published before I turned sixty was accomplished and it's great to know that it's still selling. Truth-be-told, it has succeeded far beyond my modest dreams and I am thrilled the book, with more than 35,000 copies sold, now stands as a lasting tribute to classic Maine storytelling, an artform that has meant so much to me during my life.

—John McDonald, Oct. 1, 2017

Introduction

Have you heard the one about the moose and the lobster who went into a bar? No, I didn't think so, and I'm sure you never will. If you travel around Maine looking for laughs, you'll find them—but you'll never find them linked to lines like: How many lobstermen does it take to screw in a lightbulb?

The sheer velocity of life in Maine is slower than other places, so our humor tends to be unhurried; it's allowed to take its time and develop unimpeded as it should—the way we've always liked it.

Fact is, we've never liked telling those quick one-liners they like to tell in places like New York and Las Vegas. That's one reason we don't live in those places. In Maine we tell stories from life, and feel the storyteller should take as much time as he or she needs to tell a good story right. If you find the stories funny—even if you double over laughing and have trouble breathing and need oxygen—that's fine. But you won't offend anyone—least of all the storyteller—if you just sit there and nod your head or stare at the floor waiting for the next story.

Where I grew up, the men who gathered every morning at the store in town or on the wharfs didn't tell jokes. They were storytellers, and so they told stories—yarns that had been handed down from the loggers and sailors who had worked Maine's woods and bays and spun their yarns in earlier times.

Over the years as these local narrators told their stories, the tales were doctored, adulterated, revived, repaired, reconditioned, occasionally remodeled, and even rejuvenated into the stories we love to tell today.

A Moose and a Lobster Walk into a Bar . . .

This book began as an attempt to collect some of those
fine stories and write them down, to give readers some idea
of what Maine storytelling was like years ago and what
it's like today. I felt this was a good time for such a book
because many of Maine's best local stores and wharfs are
changing or are no longer in business, and the colorful local
storytellers who performed regularly in these venues are no
longer with us.

Back in 1995 when these stories first appeared in newspapers around the state, I would put my email address
(maineauthorjohn.mcdonald@yahoo.com) at the bottom of
the column. From the first week I began receiving all kinds
of mail from all kinds of people asking all kinds of questions—most of them related to Maine. Those letters and my
responses make up another part of this book. But even here,
I always tried to answer those questions in the tradition and
the voice of a Maine storyteller.

Since everyone is a critic, I know that readers will decide,
individually, whether I succeeded or not.

Another part of this book contains my objective comments about items that appeared over the years in the newspapers I read. Here—as you will soon see—I make reasoned,
dispassionate comments about everything from a plan to
retrain Down East fishermen for "land-based careers," to
spending over $300,000—from the federal treasury—on a
trail-side outhouse.

Again, I tried to respond as if I were in a local store or on
a wharf somewhere Down East, holding a copy of the *Bangor
Daily News*.

The last chapter is called "I remember . . . ," and contains
stories inspired by events I recall from my life here in Maine.
Even here I write of these events in the voice of a storyteller,

not a historian. Most stories in this chapter are told as they happened—or as I remember them—and the people described are real.

But some of the stories in this final chapter contain composite characters, such as Uncle Abner, that I created by combining the qualities and quotes of relatives, friends and acquaintances from my past. Some of these stories also contain fictionalized events—but all characters and events are based on real people and actual events from my life.

For best results, you should take this book (after paying for it, of course) and find a good hammock set up in a quiet spot in the shade between two large trees by the water, and as you read, try to imagine the voices of those storytellers from the past.

I'd be curious to know what you think.

—John McDonald, August 2002

CHAPTER ONE

That Reminds Me of a Story

Nate Tuttle awoke one morning to find that his wife Effy had died right there in bed beside him sometime during the night. At first he wasn't sure, so he administered the foggy mirror test.

With the foggy mirror test, you hold a small mirror up to someone's nostrils for a minute or two, and if they're able to fog the mirror, they're still breathing. I'm told it's a test sometimes given to government employees to help determine their precise status with the government.

In any event, Effy Tuttle failed the foggy mirror test.

Nate was a man of few words, so rather than bother anyone with a lot of needless detail on Effy's death, he merely told the family seated in the kitchen: "You won't have to make breakfast for Mother this morning," and then he headed to the barn to build a coffin.

All morning he worked, and by noon he had fashioned a beautiful pine box for his late wife.

The two older boys, Lewis and Thurston, helped him move the coffin upstairs.

Lewis and Thurston were good boys, truth be known. Yes, they were in their thirties and still lived at home, and they were a little slow. But, they were awful hard workers, and, if properly supervised, they could be very helpful. Nate explained to the boys that he planned to place their deceased mother into the coffin, take the coffin downstairs, put it into the pickup and drive it into town to Minzey's Funeral Home.

Like many old Maine farmhouses, the old Tuttle place had a neck-breaking staircase that was steep, narrow and winding. It took Nate and the boys a while, but they managed to get the coffin up the stairs and into the bedroom. With great care, they placed Effy into the coffin, placed the lid on, nailed it shut and carried her downstairs.

Once downstairs, the two boys took over by themselves. They solemnly carried Effy, uncharacteristically laying there all peaceful-like, through the kitchen, out the back door, across the small dooryard and toward the truck. Not looking as closely as they should have at where they were going, they managed to slam the coffin into the fencepost at the edge of the dooryard.

With the jolt, Effy bolted up in the coffin and gave Nate and the boys quite a surprise, as you might imagine.

Effy, for her part, was none too pleased to wake up in a coffin. Nate began apologizing as best he could for the confusion, but knew he was in for a long siege.

Sure enough, for another twenty years Effy gave Nate almost daily reminders of the unfortunate coffin incident. But then one day, she really did die.

Being a thrifty Down Easter, Nate had kept the pine coffin in a special place in the barn. So, once again, he and his two boys—still living at home, but still good boys—carried the coffin into the house and up the stairs.

Once again, they carefully placed Effy into the coffin and began carrying her down the steep stairs.

As before, the two boys took over at the bottom of the stairs and carried the coffin through the kitchen and out the back door toward the pickup in the yard.

While the boys were going about the work of carrying their mother out of the house in a coffin for the second time in twenty years, Nate decided to take a short break. He went to the cupboard for a cup, and then over to the stove for some coffee, with the idea that he was going to sit down in the now quiet kitchen for a few minutes and relax.

But just as he was pouring the coffee, his eyes bolted wide open and he stood arrow-straight as he suddenly remembered the unfortunate coffin incident of twenty years earlier. He dropped his cup, ran to the door as quickly as he could and hollered out to his sons, "Whatever you do, boys, steer clear of that damn fencepost!"

I was sitting at the supper table enjoying a nice ham dinner the other day, when suddenly I was reminded of Billy Carpenter from back home. Poor William—not exactly the brightest bulb on the coast.

Anyway, it came to pass that one day, a distant relative died, and for some reason left Billy a prize-winning sow.

Now, as I said, Billy didn't come with a full set of rafters, meaning he would have had trouble making himself a ham and Swiss sandwich, let alone trying to figure out what to do with a prize pig.

He discussed his problem with his neighbor, Tink Billings, who told Billy he should breed the prize-winning pig and before long he'd have all kinds of piglets to sell for all kinds of money.

Billy thought that was a fine idea, but didn't know how to breed a pig. Tink told Billy to call on Merrill Minzey, who just happened to own a prize-winning boar.

"It will be easy," Tink said. "Just put your sow in your pickup, drive her down to Merrill Minzey's house, and then put her into that boar's pen."

Tink assured Billy that he wouldn't have to worry any more about it after that.

"Those two pigs will know what to do," Tink said.

So, after making arrangements, Billy took his prize sow and put her into the front seat of his pickup. He figured a prize-winning sow shouldn't be riding in the back of a pickup like an ordinary animal because there's just no telling what might happen.

Anyway, Billy drove her down to Merrill's house, where he and Merrill guided the sow down into the pen of Merrill's prize boar. The two men then went up to the kitchen for some coffee and a little conversation, and to give the pig and the boar a little privacy.

After a couple of hours, Billy went back down to the pen and retrieved his sow, put her into his pickup, and drove her home. He then put her back in her own pen and went up to his house for lunch.

Now, like I said before, Billy didn't have both his oars in the water, so when he got up the next morning he just assumed he'd see a healthy bunch of prize piglets down in the sow's pen. He was anxious to sell them as soon as he could. Instead, he found nothing in the pen but the sow standing there wagging her curly tail.

Now, Merrill had told Billy that he wouldn't be around for a few weeks, but that he would leave word with his farmhands that Billy could bring his sow back, if necessary, any time he wanted.

Undeterred by the previous morning's setback, Billy put his sow back in the pickup, drove back to Merrill's, put the pig back in the boar's pen and waited in his pickup, listening to the radio and drinking coffee.

About three hours later, Billy retrieved his sow, drove her home and again put her back in her pen.

The next morning he was even more anxious. He practically jumped out of bed and ran down to the pen to check out his valuable piglets.

Once again, he found nothing but the sow.

So again, Billy put his sow in the pickup, drove back to Merrill's farm, put her back in the boar's pen and left her for over six hours this time, figuring this was ample time to get the job done.

Next morning, he found nothing in the sow's pen but the sow. He was starting to get discouraged, but he got up and performed the same routine for the next couple of days. Finally, on the sixth morning, Billy was so tired and discouraged that he didn't even have the strength to get out of bed. He asked his wife, Ester, to go check the sow's pen for piglets.

About twenty minutes later, Ester came back upstairs with the news. She had gone down to the pen to check for piglets like Billy had asked, but found, once again, the pen empty of piglets.

"However," she added, "the sow is sitting in the front seat of your pickup waiting for you."

My Uncle Earl was a widower who lived on a beautiful farm a few miles outside of town. For as long as I can remember, he lived alone in that old house, except for his longtime housekeeper.

Early one spring, Uncle Earl started sprucing up his upstairs bathroom. He replaced the wallpaper, bought a new medicine cabinet, replaced the tile floor and painted the room from top to bottom. As a special added touch, just before he finished the makeover, he put a thick coat of paint on the toilet seat—the throne, as old Earl liked to call it.

Once he finished, he drove into town for lunch at the Mainely Food Diner.

He returned home around mid-afternoon, pulled his truck into the barn, turned off the motor and sat there in silence, thinking of what spring chore to tackle next. But soon, as he sat there in silence, he heard a strange, high-pitched noise that he couldn't quite place. He turned his earpiece up a tad, and only then could he make out what sounded like someone yelling.

He got out of the truck, stepped into the dooryard and listened again. Now Uncle Earl realized it was indeed a cry for help—and the yelling was coming from the upstairs bathroom.

Well, he ambled into the house, up the stairs and over to the bathroom door, but found the door locked. "Unlock the door," Uncle Earl yelled.

"I can't," said his distraught housekeeper. "I'm stuck to the toilet seat!"

Uncle Earl was some embarrassed, realizing he had neglected to tell the housekeeper about the freshly painted toilet seat.

"I'll get a ladder and climb through the window," Uncle Earl said. "You wait right there." Of course, that poor housekeeper couldn't have gone anywhere if she wanted to.

Uncle Earl went out into the barn and got a ladder. He then put the ladder up to the bathroom window and began climbing.

As you might expect, the housekeeper was none too pleased to see old Uncle Earl coming through the bathroom window. But this was an emergency, and she needed help getting off that seat.

Well, he tried everything he could think of. He tried pushing her and he tried pulling her. He even tried a few things with a plunger. But no matter what or how hard he tried, he couldn't get her off that toilet seat.

Eventually, he had to take the bolts off. That got her off the toilet, but the seat was still stuck fast to her backside.

So, Uncle Earl wrapped her in a wool blanket, put her in the truck, and drove her into town to see Dr. Mooney.

Both Uncle Earl and the housekeeper felt a little funny sitting there in the crowded waiting room and were sure glad when the nurse finally called them in.

The nurse, who up until that day thought she had seen it all, had the poor housekeeper get up on the examining table on her elbows and knees and then she removed the wool blanket.

Just then Dr. Mooney came into the room, and the worldly nurse turned to the good doctor and said, "Doc, look at this! Have you ever seen anything like that before?"

Dr. Mooney looked at the backside of the distraught housekeeper, thought a moment, and said, "Well, as a matter of fact, nurse, I have seen that many times before, but I can't say I've ever seen it so nicely framed."

A Moose and a Lobster Walk into a Bar . . .

One day, tired of manual labor, Tewkey Billings decided he'd get what he'd always thought of as a city job. He answered an ad in the paper from a company looking for a magazine salesman.

After an interview, they told him he had the job and was now part of the glamorous world of magazine sales. His territory would be the entire state of Maine.

The idea was to start near his home, spend the week working his way around the state, and then come home each weekend.

On his first day, he loaded his sample cases into the car and headed for a town about thirty miles away. Once there, he checked into a motel, then went out and did his first day's selling.

He returned to the motel around suppertime, and decided to call home to make sure everything was okay. His brother Liston answered the phone.

"How's everything back home, Liston?" Tewkey asked, getting right to the point of his call.

"Oh, things is okay, I guess," Liston said. After a short pause, he added, "Oh, by the way—your cat's dead."

The cat that Liston so bluntly reported dead was no ordinary cat. It happened to be a prized Maine Coon, and was probably the most valuable thing Tewkey owned.

Tewkey was some upset by Liston's report of the cat's demise. He said, "I just want you to know, Liston, that you've probably ruined my entire selling trip, giving me such bad news on the first day out."

Liston said he was sorry, but he thought Tewkey should know about his cat.

"Of course I should know," said Tewkey. "But when someone's going to be on the road a week, and they call back the first night to see how things are, you don't hit 'um right between the eyes with the bad news all at once."

"Then how should I have told you?" Liston asked, all flustered.

"Look," said Tewkey, "when someone's going to be on the road a week, and they call home the first night and you have some bad news, you say something like: 'Your cat's up on the roof, and she won't come down.' That way I don't worry, seeing's I know she's been on the roof before."

Tewkey continued, "The next night when I call, you say, 'We got your cat off the roof, but we dropped her on her back and damaged her vertebrae.' A little more serious, but I still think she'll pull through. When I call next night, you say, 'Your cat's at the vet in serious condition.' The next night, you tell me she's in a coma. And on the last night, you say my cat died quietly in her sleep. That's how you break bad news to someone who's going to be on the road for a week. Understand?"

"Yes," Liston said, all apologetic, and he promised he would never act in such a shameful way again.

Next morning, Tewkey drove on to the next town, did a good day's selling, came back to his motel and called home. Again, Liston answered.

"How are things back home?" Tewkey asked.

"Oh, things is okay, I guess," said Liston.

"That's good," said a relieved Tewkey. "And how's Mother?"

"Well, she's up on the roof," Liston said, "and she won't come down."

A Moose and a Lobster Walk into a Bar . . .

Like all good Maine Yankees, Sherm Ames knew how to squeeze a dollar, and was loathe to part with a penny if there was any good way to avoid it.

One year, he and his wife Thelma were at the Blue Hill Fair seeing the sights, when they came upon a fella giving airplane rides for five dollars each. The man stood before an old open-style airplane sitting right there on the midway as bold as brass. Sherm had never seen an airplane up close, so he was mighty curious.

However, neither Sherm nor Thelma had anything like five dollars between them, and what little they did have was reserved for fried dough. Still, they sure were impressed by the sight of that airplane.

Now the pilot wasn't doing much business on this day, so he thought he'd have a little sport with Sherm and Thelma. He said, "Listen mister, since I'm not doing much business at this time, I'll take you and your wife for a ride in my plane. And if you can sit through the entire ride without saying a word, the ride will be free."

Sherm didn't know anything about plane rides, but he knew that was no bet to make with a Down Easter. It took a lot to fluster Sherm, and he had been known to go days without uttering a word. So, Sherm took the wager. Within minutes the pilot and Sherm and Thelma were flying high above the midway. Once the pilot achieved top altitude, he began a steep, frightening nosedive. A second before potential impact, the pilot pulled out of the dive and soared back into the sky.

Sherm sat there quiet as a church mouse. It would take more than near death to get him to open his mouth.

Before long the pilot was doing loop-de-loops, fancy leaf-falls and barrel rolls and every other scary trick he could think of.

Sherm remained stone-silent. After all, a free ride was a free ride and he was not going to lose this bet over a few silly words.

Finally, the pilot realized he was just wasting fuel and he wasn't going to make Sherm talk, so he brought his plane in for a landing.

After they touched down, the pilot, one part aggravated, one part impressed, turned to Sherm and said, "Wasn't there a single time during that ride when you felt like saying anything at all?"

Sherm sat still for a moment and said, "No, not really. Well, I must admit, I did have to bite my tongue when Mother fell out, but otherwise—no!"

Like all small towns in Maine, mine has its share of churches.

We have a Catholic, Congregational, Baptist, Fundamentalist and Unitarian.

I bring the whole subject of churches up because there was quite the embarrassing incident down to the Baptist church a few weeks ago.

Hometown boy Frank Kellogg, who had just graduated from the seminary, was supposed to deliver his first sermon at the church on a recent weekend. No one is quite sure how, but the invitations went out to the wrong people, with the wrong date and time on them.

So, it wasn't surprising that when the new preacher stood in the pulpit to deliver his sermon, there was only one soul sitting out in the pews to hear it. It's not known how this lone fella happened to be there, but there he was.

Not knowing exactly what to do, and feeling a little embarrassed, the young reverend climbed down from the pulpit and walked over to the fella.

"I'm at a loss as to what to do here," said Reverend Kellogg. "I was supposed to preach my first sermon here this morning, and figured I'd have a church full of people to preach to. But you're the only one here. What do you think I should do?"

The fella, a local farmer, sat there looking down at his boots, then said, "Well, Reverend, I ain't a preacher, and I don't pretend to know nothing about it; I'm just a farmer. But I can tell you one thing: If I went down to the pasture to feed my cows, and only one cow showed up, I guess I'd feed her."

Nodding his head knowingly, the reverend said, "You are absolutely right."

With that, he spun around on his heels, and with all the determination he could muster, he marched right back up to the pulpit and started his sermon.

I'm not sure how it was found out, but it's been said that the new preacher unleashed a sermon the likes of which had seldom been heard.

They say this new reverend began preaching about the Old Testament and the New Testament; they say he preached about the Ten Commandments and the parables; they say he began preaching against sins that haven't even been committed yet, just for good measure.

For over two hours, the walls of that church rang like they'd never rung before. They say he rose to such a pitch that the paint blistered right off the walls.

And the lone farmer sat right there through it all.

Finally, the young preacher brought his first sermon to a thundering conclusion and just stood there looking out over the empty church. He swelled with pride right there in the pulpit and he didn't care who saw it.

After a minute or two, he climbed down from the pulpit and walked over to the farmer.

"Well," he said, "what did you think?"

"It's like I said, Reverend," began the farmer, "I ain't a preacher and I don't pretend to know anything about it. And like I told you, if I went down to the pasture to feed my cows and only one cow showed up, I said I'd feed her. But good Lord almighty, I wouldn't give her the whole damn load!"

Up north around Greenville, on the southern shore of Moosehead Lake, there was an attractive local woman—Thelma Harris—who was being courted by two men, a local from Jackman named Tunk Billings and a fellow from away named Jack Dawson. Thelma really liked both men and loved all the extra attention, but after a while she realized she'd eventually have to choose one or she might lose them both. The question was how to choose.

She thought, and thought, and thought. Finally, Thelma decided that a good old-fashioned Maine fishing contest was the only answer. The man who could catch the most fish in a three-day period would become her husband. Since it was winter it would have to be an ice fishing contest. Well, Tunk and Jack reluctantly agreed to the contest, the opening day was set, and they began their preparations. On the first day of the competition, Tunk, the Jackman man, returned with twelve beautiful fish. The man from away, Jack, returned with none. Not even a nibble and he had sat out on the ice all day long.

The next day, the man from away was more determined than ever to return with a mess of fish and to win the contest so that he would win the hand of Thelma, the woman of his dreams. He bought all new equipment and the best lures he could find. But when the sun set on day two, Jack once again returned to town empty-handed while Tunk returned with ten fish that were larger and more beautiful than the fish he caught the first day.

Jack just couldn't believe it. How was he catching so many fish? He figured the only way Tunk could be doing so well was that he was cheating. Jack sought advice from a local sportsman named Harold Dow, who had probably forgotten more about ice fishing than most people will ever know. At ninety-seven, Harold had forgotten a lot of other things not related to fishing, too, but I digress.

Anyway, Harold told his out-of-state friend that he should forget about trying to catch any fish on the third day of the contest because there was no way he could win now anyway. Instead of fishing, he told Jack to spend the day spying on his opponent to see if he was in fact playing by the rules or cheating. If it turned out Tunk was cheating, Harold said, he'd be disqualified, and Jack would be declared the winner and would get to marry the woman of his dreams.

Well, half-way through the third day, Jack returned to town with a big grin on his face. He went to Harold's house and told him that Tunk was indeed cheating and he had the pictures to prove it.

"Well there you go," said Harold. "You caught him and now you have him cold, so to speak. So, just what was he doing to cheat?"

"Well," said Jack. "Turns out, he was cutting holes in the ice."

A few days later Thelma and Tunk were married at the church there in Greenville.

From the time their folks died, Hollis and Thurland Bartlett lived in a camp on the family woodlot about twelve miles out of town.

The Bartlett brothers were two of the hardest working boys you'd ever want to meet, but one was as numb as a pounded thumb and the other as dumb as a haddock.

I remember being uptown at the store one morning when the Bartlett brothers arrived to do their monthly shopping. They were going up one aisle, down the other, getting all the supplies they'd need.

After a while, Hollis started moving the boxes of supplies out to the truck. On his way back inside, he stopped to look at the store's fancy window display. There, in the center of the window, was a beautiful, shiny pair of shoes priced at $150.

"That can't be," thought Hollis. "One hundred and fifty dollars for a pair of shoes?" Hollis, of course, had never paid more than five dollars for a pair of shoes in his life and that was a special pair he'd found at Marden's.

Once back inside, he said to Kendall, "There must be a mistake about those shoes in the window. They can't really cost $150?"

"No mistake," said Kendall. "I made that tag out myself. They're alligator shoes."

Hollis was dumbfounded. Alligator shoes! What will they think of next? He dragged his brother outside to see these magnificent alligator shoes.

Right then and there, the brothers decided they would sell their woodlot and all their equipment and get themselves into the alligator shoe business.

Now, I told you they were a half-bubble off plumb. The first thing they learned about the alligator business was that you couldn't raise alligators in Maine. But that was okay with them. The brothers decided if the alligators won't come to Maine, they would go to the alligators.

Before long, they had sold everything they owned, and went off to Boston where they boarded a jet for Rio de Janeiro. They planned to build a new life on the Amazon River.

Everyone in town seemed a little amused, and all figured they'd seen the last of the poor Bartlett brothers.

Then, about six months after their departure for Brazil, there was a death in the Bartlett family. One of the cousins was dispatched to fetch the brothers home for the memorial service.

The cousin rented a canoe in Rio and started paddling up the mighty Amazon.

After searching for the brothers on the river for three days with no success, he was about to declare the whole trip a failure.

Then on the fourth day, he suddenly figured he must be on their trail, because he started seeing alligators stacked up like cordwood along the river. No one stacked cordwood—whether spruce or alligator—like Hollis and Thurland Bartlett.

Shortly, the cousin came around a wide bend in the river, and what he saw almost knocked him right out of the canoe.

There on the bank he could see Thurland stacking up more alligators. And out in the middle of the mighty Amazon River he saw Hollis hand-wrestling a 21-foot alligator. It was something to behold.

He saw that the tail on that alligator was thrashing around and he saw the jaw was snapping away. But Hollis, a big fella in pretty good shape, was keeping on top of the situation.

The cousin arrived just in time to see Hollis bring his big arm around, snap that alligator's jaw shut, then cup his hand to his mouth and yell to the brother on shore: "I can tell you one thing Thurland; if this alligator ain't wearing shoes, we're going home!"

Years ago, Maine had lots of passenger trains criss-crossing and running up and down and all over the state. People from inland towns could take trains to a coastal community and from there they could board a steam packet for Boston or further Downeast. Once in Boston, they could get a train to almost anywhere in the country.

Then a man named Ford, in Highland Park, Michigan, came up with a way to make automobiles more affordable to the average person. Almost overnight the automobile went from being a luxury to being a necessity.

I barely remember the railroad days but my friend Bill Morris remembers them well and still misses them. He can't stop talking about them. He's often told me the story of the last trip he took by train from Bangor's stately railroad station. He was heading south and it was a long trip.

According to Bill, he walked into the Bangor station and simply asked the clerk for a "round-trip" train ticket. Bill got his ticket, boarded the train, and found his seat. Others boarded the train and took their seats. Soon the conductor came along and yelled toward Bill, "That bag can't be in the aisle, you've got to stow it above," and then the conductor continued along to the back of the train.

Bill didn't say anything, he just sat there, and watched the people around him and admired the scenery out the window.

A few minutes later the same fast-walking, fast-talking conductor was back and again he yelled in Bill's direction, "That damn bag can't stay in the aisle, it's got to be stowed above," and he headed toward the front of the train.

Again, Bill nodded. And continued to look out the window as the beautiful views roared by.

About fifteen minutes later, the conductor came back again. This time he was visibly agitated. He picked up the bag and says, "I already told you twice, I'm not telling you again, this bag can't stay in the aisle. He walked to the door and heaved the bag outside onto the side of the tracks. The bag hit the ground, broke open, and spread clothes and other belongings all along the side of the tracks and into the puckerbrush. It was a godawful a mess.

The conductor, satisfied that he had taken care of the problem, looked directly at Bill and said, "There now, what do you think of that!"

"Well, I wouldn't think too much of it, if it were my bag."

A few hours later Bill was getting sleepy, so he walked back to the sleeper car assigned to him. He got the last one available. And soon he was fast asleep. Just snoring away.

Long after dark, he heard a loud knock from the bed below. He heard a woman's voice call out, "Sir, are you awake?"

"I am now," Bill said. "What do you want?"

"It's quite chilly down here," said the woman. "So, I was wondering if you'd please get me another blanket to warm me up."

"Get you a blanket?" Bill said. "Tell you what, I've got a better idea and it doesn't involve me getting out of bed. Let's just pretend we are an old married couple."

"Well, that sounds very interesting," the woman said. "Let's pretend we are married. Will you please help me get warm?"

"Sure, just get up and get your own damn blanket," he said. "And you'll be fine."

With all the tourists starting to pour into Maine at the beginning of summer, I suddenly got real homesick and decided to take a trip down home to Cherryfield to see what was going on.

What you have to understand about Cherryfield is that when everything is going along as usual, there usually isn't a whole lot going on. That is just the way the folks down there like it, and why I still like to go down there for a visit now and then.

The town manager, Alex Davis, sets the pace in town. He's been managing things there for almost thirty years now. They say he also manages to take a nap every afternoon around two.

Anyway, Alex got a pretty little needlepoint sign to put up on the wall behind his desk in his office, and that sign sort of sums up his whole town-managing career.

It says, "So little time, so little to do."

So I headed down to Augusta, took Route 3 across to Belfast, joined Route 1 in Belfast and started heading Down East.

Along about the other side of Bucksport, the Maine Department of Transportation gang was into some serious orange cone placement, shovel leaning and road rearranging. This led to a wholesale detouring of traffic.

It got so bad, I finally couldn't tell where it was I was coming from, or where it was I was supposed to be going to.

About that time, I came to an intersection and pulled over to get my bearings. In the field next to the road was an old-timer raking. I called to him and asked how to get back to Route 1.

The old gentleman slowly put down his rake. Even more slowly he mopped his brow, and walked very slowly toward the road.

Once he got to the car, it didn't take him too long to get me straightened out, direction-wise.

I thanked the old guy, but before I drove off, I couldn't help but ask him a few questions—just like those tourists we are always complaining about.

"You're kinda old to be out here raking hay in the hot sun alone, aren't ya?" I asked.

He looked me dead in the eye and said, "Not that it's any of your business, but I'm barely 64. And normally my father would be here helping me, but he's in the barn fixing the tractor."

"Your father? How old's he?" I continued.

He said, "He's 83. And again, it's none of your business, but my grandfather would normally be out here helping too, but he couldn't make it this morning."

"That's too bad," I said. "Ill, is he?"

"Ill? He's never been sick a day in his life."

There was a long silence.

Finally, I said, "Well, I'm glad to hear your grandfather isn't ill. So, where is he?"

"On his honeymoon!" he answered.

"His honeymoon? You can't be serious," I said. "How old did you say this grandfather of yours was?"

"I didn't say, but the man is 104 years old," he said.

I shook my head in disbelief "Well, now, isn't that ridiculous? Why would a man 104 years old want to run off and get married?"

"Well, that's the rub right there," he said. "He didn't want to. He had to."

Mainers are nothing, if not frugal. They know how to squeeze a dime, or a nickel, or a penny. One time, these two old farmers, Kevin Peters and Brian David, went to the county fair and proceeded to eat lots and lots and lots of fried food. After about the third batch of fried dough, both of the old farmers had to find a privy at the same time.

A Moose and a Lobster Walk into a Bar . . .

This was back in the day and the only "bathroom" at the fair was one of those long outhouses that featured more than one hole. So after they both finished their business, Kevin stood up, and as he did, his spare change fell out of his pocket and dropped right down through the hole. Kevin stood there for a minute just staring back down the hole where he had just been sitting. Finally, he started taking off his shoes, his overalls, his shirt, and so forth until he was stark naked.

Brian stood there, somewhat amazed. He grew even more bewildered as he watched Kevin grab his pants, reach in the pocket, take out a five-dollar bill and promptly drop it down the hole.

This was all too much for Brian.

"Have you gone crazy?" he yelled out. "What in tarnation did you do that for?"

Kevin paused for a minute before answered what he felt was a stupid question.

"Well," he said. "I sure as hell ain't going down there just to get back a handful of change."

The older folks back home like to tell the story about the first motorcycle ever seen in Down East Maine. Hometown boy Walter Merrill had joined the army, and when he came back home for a visit one time he brought along a bright and shiny new Harley Davidson motorcycle.

Most of the people in town had seen pictures of these so-called motorcycles, in magazines and newspapers, but most folks had never seen a real one up close. So when Walt came rumbling through town and parked his big, bad, shiny, new bike in front of the store, it drew quite a crowd.

Lots of folks thought it was kind of funny that Walt should be the first in town to get himself something like a motorcycle. Walt wasn't on what we might call today the "cutting edge" of anything, except maybe a buck saw. And older folks remembered Walt could barely ride a bicycle until he was almost old enough to shave.

After showing his Harley to the folks in front of the store, someone suggested to Walt that he might ride his impressive vehicle out to Wink Dalrimple's place, to see how old Wink would react to such a contraption. Walt agreed it would be fun, so, after taking a few hair-raising turns around the town square, he headed out to Wink's place.

Now, Wink Dalrimple and his wife, Bessie, lived about as far out in the country as you could live and still be somewhere within the boundaries of the state of Maine.

He came to town about three times a year, whether he liked to or not, and most of the time he made it real plain to all that he didn't like to. Until that day, you probably would have said of Wink that he was as cantankerous and anti-social a fella as you were likely to meet anywhere north of Boston. And Wink was considered the charmer in the Dalrimple family.

Folks in town put up with Wink because he was part of what those professors at the university like to call the "fabric of the community."

Walt headed out to Route 9, the airline, and took a turn onto the tote road that leads to Wink's place.

Wink was sitting on his front porch, smoking a pipe and looking through *The Saturday Evening Post* when Walt came racing up the drive on his roaring, spitting and snorting Harley.

Without hesitating, Wink, not one quick to panic, dashed into the house, took down his hunting rifle, came back out on the porch, and blasted away at the motorcycle.

Well, the motorcycle went flying toward one side of Wink's driveway and sailed right into the pucker brush, and Walt went flying toward the opposite side of the driveway and into another patch of pucker brush.

Wink's wife Bessie, who'd heard all the commotion, came to the screen door to watch the whole thing. When things quieted down a bit, Bessie said, "Did you get that critter, Wink?"

"I don't know," Wink said, "but at least it let go of Waltah!"

I was down at the store the other day having coffee at the counter with a contingent of local scholars, commentators and observers, when Charlie Farron, our local sheriff's depu-

ty, walked in and joined us.

Now, I don't know what kind of work you do, but I know there are few jobs tougher these days than the job of enforcing the law throughout this land.

When he took on his policing job 26 years ago, Charlie thought he was just getting into law enforcement—meaning he thought he'd be doing just police work (and, of course, waiting for that good pension). But these days, Charlie says the police also have to act as marriage counselors, babysitters, substance abuse experts, and public relations officials.

One reason I like Charlie Farron is because he's always got a good story. The other day, Charlie told me about the fella he stopped recently for having a headlight out. As Charlie approached the car, he noticed the fella wasn't wearing his seat belt.

When Charlie reminded the fella that Maine law now required the wearing of seat belts, the man got all in a huff and said, "Officer, I know all about the seat belt law, thank-you-very-much, and I had my belt on, but just now unbuckled it to get my driver's license."

Well, Charlie didn't know what to do but ask the fella's wife who, according to Charlie, looked like an honest Maine woman.

"Ma'am," said Charlie, "I'll let you settle this for us here. As far as you know, was your husband wearing his seat belt, or not?"

The wife said, "Officer, I've been married to Barney here a long time. And if there's one thing I've learned in all those years, it's never argue with him when he's been drinking."

They tell the story along the coast about the couple—Hollis and Ella Eaton—who had been lobstering

together since before they were married.

Back in the early days, Hollis, who wasn't as romantic as some lobstermen, would ask Ella to go lobstering with him instead of asking her on a more traditional date, like smelting or getting the jumbo platter at the fried fish shack.

Being the agreeable type, Ella went lobstering. Rather than just sit in the boat and watch, she'd fill the bait bags while Hollis hauled the traps and took out the counters. It was a romance just made for Down East.

Eventually, they were married and became true partners. Every morning, Hollis and Ella would go lobstering together.

They didn't say much during the day. In fact, they barely acknowledged each other. Hollis would haul the traps, take out the counters and slide the traps along the gunwale to Ella, who would take out the shorts, bait the traps and set them back. They were very strict about their routine and wouldn't deviate come hell or high water. And like, good Down Easters, they wanted every dime they could get.

One day, the two were out lobstering when a rough sea came up. Hollis and Ella just kept right on working, barely noticing what was going on around them—same as usual.

At one point, a large wave broke over the stern of their boat, and took Ella right overboard.

Not realizing anything was wrong, Hollis kept right on lobstering. He had slid three or four traps down the gunnels before he discovered that Ella was gone.

Being a relatively sharp man, he concluded right quick that Ella must have gone overboard. He was some upset, especially since he still had over ninety traps left to haul.

He didn't like it much and was kind of miffed at Ella for taking off, but for the first time in years, he managed all by himself. He hauled the remaining traps, took out the keepers and shorts, baited them all, and set every trap. He then brought his boat in, sold the lobsters, got bait for the next morning, took the boat out to the mooring, washed it down, rowed into his dock and went up to the house and made himself a coffee. Once he did all that, he felt it was the proper time to call the Coast Guard.

As I said, you've got to understand that Hollis was a man of habit, and not even this tragedy could break him of a routine—he knew that might jinx him and cause something bad to happen.

By now it had been a few hours since his dear Ella had gone overboard, but Hollis described her to the Coast Guard fella as best as he could remember.

The Coast Guard fella said if they found anything, Hollis would be the first to know.

The next day, Hollis got a call from the Coast Guard. One of their patrol boats had found a body fitting Ella's description. She was found floating in a bed of kelp, just offshore. When they hauled her aboard the patrol boat, she even had seven or eight lobsters attached to her.

"What would you like us to do with the body, Mr. Eaton?" the Coast Guard fella asked solemnly.

"Well," said Hollis, "knowing how much that woman loved catching lobsters and how hard it is find bait, I think Ella would want you to take those lobsters off and set her again."

When the weather gets cold back home, folks start thinking about their health. Most try to schedule a physical every five years or so whether they really need it or not.

This was made clear to me during a visit back home this past summer. A fella not lucky enough to work in the health area told me his business was so bad that even people who didn't pay had stopped buying.

But doctoring is thriving.

My former neighbor, Thurland Pease, told about a recent visit to his doctor—Dr. Dinsmore. The good doctor examined Thurland up one side and down the other, and back again twice just for good measure.

When he got all done, he said, "Well, Thurland, you seem to be in pretty good shape. How do you feel?"

Thurland said, "Doc, I've never felt better in my life."

Doc Dinsmore said, "That's good, Thurland. And how's your regularity?"

"Doc, you see that clock of yours on the wall?" Thurland said. "You could set that clock by my regularity. Six-thirty, every single morning."

Doc Dinsmore nodded approvingly and made a notation in Thurland's file, then said, "Well, Thurland, that's very good."

"Well, Doc, it isn't really that good," Thurland said. "I'm never up 'til seven."

Old Judge Pomeroy was considered a hard judge. He would dole some harsh punishment on those who came before his court if he felt a lesson was necessary.

One time this old fella, Benjamin Dawes was caught fishing without a license. The local police had caught him down in the brook a few times, in the lake a few times, and in the ocean a few times, and had let him off with just a warning each time.

Finally, he pushed his luck a little too far and the police hauled him into court to stand before old Judge Pomeroy. The judge, after he heard about all the warnings, handed down a fine of a whopping $200 dollars or three nights in the county jail. Old Ben wasn't too pleased by the verdict. Two hundred was all the money he had, but he couldn't bear the thought of spending time in jail. And his wife would kill him. So after Ben paid the fine, he asked the judge for a signed receipt.

Judge Pomeroy was a little taken aback.

"Well, sure, you can have a receipt. But what's the matter—don't you trust me?"

Old Ben looked the judge square in the eye and said, "Oh, sure, I trust ya' Judge, but you and I are getting up in years, and before long we are both going to be meet St. Peter at the pearly gates. When I get there ole Peter is going to ask me if I have ever committed a crime, and I can't say, 'No,' so I'll have to say, 'Yes.' Then he's going to ask if I have ever been to court, and again, I'll have to say 'Yes.' Then he will most assuredly ask me if I paid my fine, and if I don't have that receipt as proof, they are going to have to look all over hell to ask Judge Pomeroy."

Maine is the only state of the lower 48 that borders only one other state.

This creation of colonial politics and clever surveying means that New Hampshire is the only state we Mainers

share a border with. And as with any neighbor, there is
sometimes a little bickering.

A frequent skirmish between Maine and New Hampshire
concerns ownership of a piece of land in the Piscataqua
River—a pile of silt and fill that has a shipyard built on it—
the Portsmouth Naval Shipyard.

From time to time, New Hampshire officials file a suit
trying to lay claim to the whole of that island and the shipyard on it.

Maine officials are a tad upset with this neighborly dispute, mostly because they think the sand pile in the river
belongs to the people of Maine.

If this piece of land was just a pile of silt, of course, we
probably wouldn't care who claimed it. But the shipyard
makes it a pretty valuable piece of property. Not only that,
but everyone who works there at the shipyard is required to
pay income taxes to Maine.

This isn't the first time, and it probably won't be the last,
that we argue with our neighbor about the exact location of
the border. A few years ago, a team of surveyors was hired by
Maine and New Hampshire to try to set the border once and
for all.

One day they were working in Oxford County, and after
spending a day going through swamps and fields and pucker
brush, they realized that a farm on the border was not in
Maine at all, but was actually in New Hampshire.

One of the surveyors was given the task of telling the
owner the news. The surveyor fella was a little concerned
because he didn't know how the farm's owner would take
to being told his farm had just moved from one state to
another. He walked up to the farmhouse, called "hello" a few
times, and finally an elderly gentleman came to the door.

"Sir," he said, "I'm with the survey team straightening out the border here and after surveying through your farm, we discovered that your place isn't in Maine at all—it's actually in New Hampshire."

The old man looked a little stunned at first, but then said, "Well, thank you, young fella, for that news, and thank the good Lord, too. You know, I was just sitting here wondering how I was going to make it through another Maine winter."

Despite what you may think, I haven't always been part of the glamorous world of journalism. For years, I was part of the slightly less glamorous, but infinitely more important, world of sales.

At one time in my life, I covered the state of Maine for a company that made some of the most useless things ever to come out of a factory. The company had an entire line of little-needed and even less-desired merchandise.

And I was their man in Maine.

One time up in Aroostook County, I stopped for directions from a farmer, who was just leading his prize bull out to pasture. Following accepted custom, I began by observing what a fine-looking animal he had.

The farmer agreed it was a splendid bull, and began telling me how he almost got rid of it.

He said the bull had suddenly become impotent, and was therefore worthless to his whole breeding program there at the farm.

He called the vet, who rushed right over to check out the bull. The farmer said the good animal doctor gave him some powerful medicine that he promised would cure the bull's problem in 48 hours—or less.

"Well," said the farmer, "you should have seen this bull after a day or two of that special medicine. He was back on the job, performing his duties better than ever. It was a spectacular recovery, there's no other way to describe it," the farmer said.

"Isn't that something," I said. "I wonder what a special medicine like that is made of?"

"I don't know," said the farmer, "but it tastes to me like licorice."

I was reading a story in the paper the other day about a couple Down East who were celebrating their 75th wedding anniversary with a party at the Grange Hall. And that reminded me of a story I heard about a couple I knew back home—Arthur and Mabel Bunker—who also celebrated a 75th anniversary with all kinds of friends and relations.

The way I heard the story, this was one of the biggest parties ever held in our town, and by the time it was all over the poor old couple could barely move. They were just sitting in their comfortable parlor, resting.

After a while, the husband thought it a good time to ask his dear wife about some items he had recently come across in the attic. He told his dear Mabel that he had been upstairs a few days before, looking over the many relics of their long and happy life, when he happened to open an old steamer trunk and there on top were some curious items.

In the trunk, on top of his wife's now-brittle wedding gown, there were three ears of corn and twenty-five one-dollar bills. He said he'd left the items undisturbed but had to admit that he was "some curious" as to what the corn and the money were doing there in the old trunk.

Mabel's cheeks turned a shade of pink that Arthur hadn't seen in years. She slowly turned away from her husband and just looked out the window into the backyard for a while. Then, ever so slowly, she turned back and looked straight at her husband, and finally, but haltingly, said, "Well, Arthur, I hadn't planned to talk about things like this, but I suppose, this being our 75th wedding anniversary, and after all the good times we've been talking about today, it might be about time I told you about those curious items you came across in the attic."

At that point, Arthur wasn't sure he wanted to hear any more, but with her odd remarks, Mabel had made him even more curious, so he just sat there.

"Over the seventy-five years of our happy marriage," Mabel began, "whenever I indiscreetly wandered off the 'straight and narrow' and was, well, kinda 'unfaithful,' I always went up in the attic afterwards and placed a single ear of corn on top of my wedding gown in that old steamer trunk."

Arthur could hardly believe what his dear wife was saying. He was completely stunned by Mabel's shameful revelations. But as the couple sat there in the fading light, eventually Arthur softened. Soon, he was recalling the early years of their marriage when he'd spent so much of his time at sea. He remembered how lonely he had been during that time, and thought that that same loneliness must have been too much for his dear wife Mabel. He concluded that those long stretches at sea must have been when Mabel committed her "indiscretions."

It had all been so long ago and now seemed so far away that Arthur didn't feel the least bit angry toward his loving wife and her misguided actions. He was willing to forgive and completely forget Mabel's three dalliances.

But first, there was just one more detail he wanted to ask Mabel about.

Arthur said, "First, I want to thank you, my dear, for being so forthright and honest. You certainly have explained the mystery of the three ears of corn in the steamer trunk, but there's still the matter of the twenty-five one-dollar bills. If you don't mind my asking: What's the story with those bills?" Arthur asked.

"Well," Mabel began, "it's like I just told you, Arthur, every time I went 'astray,' I always remembered to place a single ear of corn in the steamer trunk on top of my wedding gown. And whenever I had enough corn to fill a bushel basket, I'd sell it for a dollar a bushel."

They still tell the story down at the store about the fella from New Jersey who came to Maine to see what it was like to spend a week in the great north woods.

This New Jersey fella hired himself a Maine guide by answering an ad in a sportsman's magazine. Turns out the ad was placed by my neighbor, Murray Seavey, the one who told me the story.

Murray picked this fella up at the Bangor International Airport, loaded his fancy, new gear into the truck and headed to his camp up to Township 10.

As they drove along, the New Jersey fella looked out the window at the miles and miles of woods and began to wonder just what it was he was getting himself into. Being born and raised in the city he'd never spent much time around trees—at least not as many as he now saw speeding by the window of the truck.

For years he had talked about having what people in the city call, "a wilderness experience," or what Mainers call, "a trip to camp."

And now, here he was.

When they got to camp Murray got right to work setting things up. By now the New Jersey fella was so nervous about being in the wild woods of Maine that he was afraid to let Murray out of his sight and followed him around camp like a puppy.

At one point Murray finally turned to him and said, "Look, why don't you make yourself useful and take that bucket down to the spring and get us some water, while I finish building us a fire in the stove for supper."

Wanting to be agreeable, the fella took the bucket, went out the door and down the path to the spring.

Five minutes later he's back, he's as white as a ghost and the bucket in his hand is rattling away.

Murray took one look at him and said, "What in the world is wrong with you?"

The fella from New Jersey said, "Well, I went down to the spring like you asked me, and when I got there I saw what must have been a 300-pound black bear standing right up to his waist in the spring!"

"And that's what's got you all scared to death?" Murray asked, scratching his beard.

"Well, yes," said the New Jersey fella, a little annoyed at Murray's reaction.

"Let me tell you something," said Murray. "I guarantee you that black bear was as scared of you as you were of him!"

"Is that true?" asked the fella, now a tad embarrassed.

"That is absolutely true," said Murray, emphatically.

"In that case," said the fella, with a little chuckle, "that spring water isn't fit to drink, now, anyway."

CHAPTER TWO

Black Flies, Mud Season, and Summer Complaints

Now that the tourists around here are as thick as flies round a bait barrel, Maine's largest industry begins to come alive—an industry as important to our state's economy as paper mills and Bath Iron Works combined.

The tourist industry, you ask?

Naaah. The tourist industry earns pennies compared to the big bucks pumped into our state by this vast economic engine—an industry that affects the lives of every man, woman and child in our state. I'm referring, of course, to the YSI—the Yard Sale Industry—which is overseen by the powerful Yard, Flea and Garage Retailers Association and its lobbyist in Augusta.

In sheer tonnage, nothing can hold a candle (or a battered kerosene lamp) to our lawn sale industry.

As I write this, tons of overpriced treasures are being hauled out of tens of thousands of homes onto countless acres of lawn throughout the state. Yard sales are blossoming like ragweed.

It doesn't matter what you call them: lawn sales, garage sales, attic sales or barn sales. They are all part of the same

industry and are based on the same idea: Get out on a lawn somewhere and sell something—anything!

If you go to enough YFAGRA events you'll begin to marvel at how this giant industry works.

For example, you'll be at a YFAGRA branch in Bristol, you'll stop, scratch your head and say, "Didn't I see this Combination Hot Dog Steamer-Wallpaper Remover last week in Bethel?"

That's one of the many things the YFAGRA does. It moves tons of pricey junk, an item at a time, from places like Bethel to places like Bristol and lots of places in between. But it also makes lots of non-taxed money in the process.

When the industry is really humming it also manages to sell hundreds of tons of yard-sale items to tourists who can't wait to strap their treasures to their cars and haul them out of state.

There has been some evolution of the YFAGRA over the years. It once relied largely on our venerable town dumps before they were replaced by "transfer stations."

In the old days a fella would load up his pickup and head for the town dump to heave everything down over the bank. Then he would stand there beside his truck and scan the dump for treasures.

Eventually, he'd spot a beautiful old bathtub, just perfect for watering the horse he planned to buy. Into the truck would go the tub.

Then he'd spy some old barn boards for that deck he planned to build, an oil drum for starting his outboard each spring (when he actually got an outboard), an engine block from an old Chevy that would make a perfect mooring for the boat he was planning to build come winter, and a beautiful family entertainment center that looked like it just needed a little tinkering.

He would end up hauling twice as much stuff out of the dump as he hauled into it. And all of it, after cluttering up his dooryard for five or ten years, would become prime yard sale material. Sadly, all that changed when the dumps closed.

But because of its sheer size and power, our native yard sale industry took the hit, adjusted to the changing times, retooled and became stronger than ever.

It's still Maine's most important industry and anyone can get a piece of the action. There's no large capital investment required, no training necessary. You don't even need an 800-number.

Just drag some stuff out onto the lawn and start selling.

Depending on when you read this we could be in the middle of another one of those early-spring heat waves or we could've had a thick layer of frost on our windshields this morning and awakened to the sound of the furnace humming a familiar tune.

On a recent spring day when the thermometer unexpectedly shot up into the 80s, I sprang into action and ran into the kitchen. There I made myself a nice cold pitcher of lemonade and took it onto the back deck so I could sit in the shade and look at the river and think about what it was I should be doing on such a hot day.

I'm not sure what was in that lemonade but before long I was planning my first yard sale of the new season—and there wasn't even a tourist or a black fly in sight. When I finished the lemonade I wandered into the barn to look over the pile of useless junk (I mean practical items), that we had been collecting for just such an important annual event.

Right off, I noticed my ingenious Pocket Fisherman. Remember those clever things?

Somehow after watching their slick ads on TV, I became convinced that the reason I was not catching any fish wasn't because I had no clue as to what I was doing.

No, siree.

My failure as a fisherman was directly related to the fact that I had one of those long, old-fashioned fishing poles that were difficult to transport. If only I had a versatile pole that could fit easily into a small carrying case or my glove compartment—or better yet, my *pants pocket*.

Well, I sent for a Pocket Fisherman and things sure did change. I was transporting that pole around easier than I had ever transported a fishing pole in my life. It was fantastic.

But my fishing skills never improved; and after a few weeks of carrying my Pocket Fisherman on my belt and in my pocket and then my glove compartment, I got sick of the stupid thing and took it out to the barn.

The next thing I came across was the smokeless ashtray we bought a few years back after seeing those creative ads on television. In fact, we ended up buying half a dozen of them since they only cost $9.98 each—plus a modest shipping and handling fee.

Did you ever see one? Those crafty smokeless ashtrays had tiny fans in them that sucked cigar and cigarette smoke right out of the air and into a special little chamber. They worked like a charm until that inside part got crammed with smoke— and then they were just like any other smelly ashtray.

Sitting near the smokeless ashtrays in this pile of gems was my old Ronco Bottle and Jar Cutter.

Mother and I saw those on TV and agreed it was just what we needed to take all our old bottles and jars and turn them into "decorative glassware, centerpieces and thousands of other useful things."

It wasn't until I bought one, unwrapped it and looked at it that I came to my senses and realized that the last thing I needed was a thousand other glass things around the house, decorative or otherwise, so I sure didn't need the Ronco Bottle and Jar Cutter. My loss will be someone else's gain, because even though it cost me a cool $7.77 (plus a modest shipping and handling fee), I'd be willing to part with my bottle and jar cutter for, say, $5.

Way over in the corner behind my old set of Ginsu knives and my Inside the Eggshell Scrambler was one of my first television purchases ever—the Veg-O-Matic. It's considered by many to be the greatest food appliance ever hyped on the airwaves of this great country. Unfortunately, we could never get it to work for us.

I can hear you saying, "But John, the Veg-O-Matic could slice a whole potato into uniform slices with one motion and you just turned the ring to go from thin to thick slices."

You don't have to tell me. I know all about it. And after making hundreds of French fries in a minute, you could change from slicing to dicing to make mounds of diced onions.

Believe me, I know.

Once we got it we realized how rarely it was that we had the urge to go—in seconds—from slicing to dicing. Nor did we really like piles of French fries and mounds of onions all over the kitchen.

So, everything's gotta go. A bunch of people will walk away from our first yard sale with stuff that'll sure "make great Christmas gifts."

Please hurry, though—supplies are limited.

Back in the fifties when I was a kid, folks used to refer to our summer visitors as "summer complaints." It's hard to imagine what the good people of Maine were thinking in those dark ages. Today, thanks to folks like the ones at the Maine Office of Tourism, we know better.

Over the years, those of us who depend on tourist dollars for a good chunk of our incomes have become more sensitive about the feelings of our summer visitors. In these enlightened times we would never use such an insensitive expression as *summer complaint*, unless first looking around to see if any flatlanders were listening.

In the old days, it was common for a restaurant owner to say to a table full of summer guests something like, "You summer complaints have been sitting here looking at our ocean view long enough. It's Bingo Night and I feel lucky, so pay up and get out." Today, in our more enlightened age, restaurateurs are much more likely to say something like, "Would you folks like some recycled paper cups so you can finish those coffee refills out in our spacious parking lot?"

To show how far we have progressed in our attitudes toward tourists in Maine, I'd like to instruct our summer visitors on some of the more unique words in the Maine vocabulary so they can appear more aware and less bewildered when conversing with natives.

Since this is a wholesome family publication, I will, of course, avoid such expressions as "Tighter than a bull's #@% in fly season," and concentrate on words that are considered in general use.

Pucker brush: This is any kind of green growth along the side of a Maine road. Rather than try to be specific and use a bunch of fancy tree-hugger words, a Mainer will say, "That fella just pitched some trash right into the pucker brush."

Dooryard: I've had people from away call me on the radio and ask what a "dooryard" is. It's one of those words we've used so long, we've never sat down to lay out exactly what it means. The best I can figure, a dooryard is that part of your backyard that is around your back door or visible from your back door. So you'll hear a Mainer say, "I was standing there in my dooryard when I saw Harold throw something into the pucker brush."

Cunnin': This is a word Mainers use to describe something, or someone, that others from away might describe as being "cute." Since a real Mainer would not use the word "cute" (and wouldn't admit it if he did), the word cunnin' is in much more common usage. Therefore, you might hear someone say, "I was standing there in the pucker brush looking over toward Harold's dooryard, when someone came out the door with a little baby that was some cunnin'."

Ugly: In Maine this word has nothing to do with someone's physical appearance, but rather with disposition. Hence, you'll often hear someone say something like, "As I walked out of the pucker brush toward the cunnin' baby in

Harold's dooryard, I noticed it was Harold himself holding the baby, and didn't he look ugly about something."

Well, I hope that that helps all the summer complaints ... I mean blessed summer visitors.

With tourist season in full swing, it's time to review some basic, time-honored Maine customs long practiced in those tourist circles, which, as we know, can sometimes be more confusing than Maine's traffic circles.

Most of us come in contact with tourists when they stop to ask us for directions. That's also when they're the least dangerous and you can have the most fun with them.

Which leads to Custom Number One:

Mainers never say one word more than necessary when giving directions. Tourists think we're people of few words. We shouldn't disappoint them.

There was a tourist from Massachusetts who went into a country store up north to get his bearings from the clerk. He said, "If I take the road to the left in front of the store, where will I end up?"

The clerk thought a minute then said, "Mooselookmeguntic."

"Okay," said the fella from Massachusetts, "what if I took the road to the right, where does that go?"

"Mattawamkeag," said the clerk.

"And if I took the road that goes straight?" said the fella.

Without skipping a beat the clerk said, "Wytopitlock."

Annoyed, the tourist said, "Well, thank you very much."

He left the store, got back in his Volvo and his wife said, "Well, do you know where we are now?"

"Heck, no!" the man said. "Guy in there doesn't even speak English!"

Back home, giving directions was more than just a diversion; it was a well-honed craft.

Which leads to Custom Number Two:

Mainers don't just give out information to the tourist, we try to get a little information in return. Which brings to mind the time I was sitting on Dickey Merrill's front porch and another couple from Massachusetts stopped for directions to Bangor.

Dickey, a direction-giver of world-class standing, started right off giving one direction after another. The wife, on the passenger side, wrote it all down. (That's a tourist—get everything in writing.)

When Dickey was done, she wound up her window and off they went in their Saab.

Five minutes later, the same couple in the same car stopped in front of the house again.

You see, Dickey had directed them up one side of town, across the river, back down the other and across again, in one complete circle.

When the wife finally realized what he'd done, she wound the window down again and proceeded to give Dickey a tongue-lashing so severe it started to blister the paint on the front of his house. Dickey hadn't heard such strong language since the last church social.

When she was all done, she demanded an apology from him for directing them like that around the town.

Dickey said, "Listen de-ah, I just wanted to make sure you could follow directions, before I wasted my time directing you all the way to Bangor."

You can have the most glorious August day of the summer going on around you—with cool breezes off the sparkling water and deep blue skies stretching as far as the eye can see—and you can be making plans for sailing and swimming and ball games and picnics, when suddenly the whole day can be ruined with one innocent flick of the wrist as you flip a newspaper page. It has happened to me many a year.

In the days of my lost youth, I'd be sitting on the family porch on some August morning reading the comics or fretting about the Red Sox, and just as casually as you please, I'd turn the page and get hit right between the eyes with a full-page color advertisement for a "Back-to-School" sale.

I would get pretty ill just looking at such mean-spirited ads filled with smiling kids—the kind who looked like they just couldn't wait to get this summer vacation business out of the way so they could get back to where they really wanted to be—school.

It was bad enough that the dreaded school days would come along eventually, but those days in the month of August—the month of warm summer days and cool summer nights—it was off-limits to talk of school as far as I was concerned.

By any measure, it was still school vacation and therefore no time at all to ruin things with thoughtless newspaper ads about returning to the dreary place we fled in June.

Once the back-to-school business started, summer was never quite the same. After you saw one of those ads everything else about the remaining days of summer was tainted, and just that much gloomier around the edges.

Then my mother would decide it was time to pack us kids into the station wagon and head to town so we could load up on school clothes and supplies. Although the school year began when it was still technically summer, our school clothes in those days were always the kind of rugged, sensible clothes made for fall here in Maine. Mother would always buy piles of flannel shirts, heavy corduroy pants and lots of wool socks.

It never failed that the first week of school always included some of the warmest days of the year. On those days, the afternoon sun would beat down something fierce on all that flannel and corduroy and wool. The new outfits always made me itch and sweat up a storm as I shuffled sadly along the sidewalk loaded with books and homework. I trudged through town dreaming about the long-lost days of summer.

I bring up all this unpleasant business about back-to-school sales not just because many of our little scholars here in Maine have begun another school year, but also because of something I read in the newspaper.

Since leaving my school days behind and achieving something akin to adult status I no longer dread the start of another school year. These days I look forward to this time of year when the hordes of tourists loaded with their school-aged kids and luggage and pets and Chinese-made souvenirs head south down the turnpike, and we Mainers can once again get back to whatever it was we were doing last June just before all the downtown parking spaces got taken. Fact is, now that I don't have to go back to school anymore, fall has become my favorite season.

A Moose and a Lobster Walk into a Bar . . .

So you can imagine my surprise recently when, with an innocent flick of the wrist, I turned the page of my newspaper and came across an article about that group in Augusta in charge of promoting tourism here in Maine. Apparently, these people are spending what seems to me like a lot of tax money on an ad campaign aimed at getting those hordes of people who just left us around Labor Day to turn around and come back up here again so they can stand around and "Oooh" and "Ahhh" at Maine's autumn.

Now, I have nothing against people from away—"leafers"—coming around and making a big fuss over our colorful autumn leaves (as long as they leave lots of money behind). Folks have done it around here for years. Occasionally, I do it myself. It's just that the whole ad project reminded me of those summer days years ago when I would turn the page of a newspaper and get hit right between the eyes with those ads for "Back-to-School" sales.

What an unpleasant flashback. I haven't felt this queasy in years.

Suddenly, it was as if I were wearing too-small corduroys, flannels and wools, and sitting at a beat-up desk that was bolted to the floor in Miss Fickett's overheated fifth grade classroom.

Ever notice how when you sit around your woodstove in the wintertime looking at the family photo album and thinking about warmer weather, you start conjuring up fond memories of all the good times you and the family had during past summers at the lake and at your folks' place on the coast or up-country at Baxter State Park? Ever notice how your memories never include thoughts of pesky mosquitoes, black flies, midges, biting houseflies or ticks?

It doesn't matter that we don't think about insects and flies during the cold weather because as soon as the outside temperature gets above 60 for any length of time and we move outdoors to enjoy ourselves, the mosquitoes and midges and black flies and houseflies and ticks descend on us like the plague.

I only mention this because I want you to remember as you go about your business this spring buying all sorts of useful spring items, that a portion of the sales tax you're paying goes to help support the Maine Department of Conservation's Insect and Disease Management Division.

You're probably sitting there at the kitchen table scratching your head right now and mumbling something like: "I didn't even know we had an 'Insect and Disease Management Division' in our Department of Conservation." Well, we do. And it's a government job, so it must be pretty darned important.

I understand from my extensive research (a phone call) that the folks there are doing everything humanly possible to keep the pesky mosquito, black fly, midge, biting housefly and tick population around here under control.

According to the information they sent me from the home office, there's good news and bad news in bug country. The bad news: There are roughly 37 different species of mosquitoes, 43 species of black flies, 40 species of biting midges, 76 species of houseflies and deer flies and 14 species of ticks in our neck of the woods. The good news: Only 20 percent of the species in each group bites humans.

A Moose and a Lobster Walk into a Bar . . .

If you've ever been covered with welts from mosquitoes, black flies and midges, that "good news" is like telling a person who's just been mugged that the the crime rate is way down. Here in Maine most of the nuisance mosquitoes are of the *Aedes* sp. persuasion. I don't know exactly what the name means, but I'm told that entomologists, also known as bug experts, sit around their offices and think up names like *Aedes* sp. so the rest of us won't know exactly what they're talking about.

Bug experts group mosquitoes on the basis of where they breed. Some mosquitoes breed in the woods and others can't get romantic unless they're in salt marsh pools. A few species like to breed in small stagnant ponds or swampy areas; and others breed in water that has accumulated in discarded tires or containers like cemetery urns. (That must be where that old mosquito line, "Your urn, or mine?" came from.)

My advice to you at this point is this: If you have a bunch of discarded tires or cemetery urns in your yard—and who doesn't?—get rid of them before that cookout this weekend and replace them with something clever, like one of those mushroom-shaped lawn ornaments that look like someone's backside.

The most upsetting thing I learned while doing all this research on the breeding habits of mosquitoes and other insects is the answer to the question: "Why do mosquitoes bite us in the first place?"

I had always heard that only the female bites, but I never knew why. What I learned was that all mosquitoes get most of their nutrition from flower nectar and plant sap. Only females need our blood to obtain the protein they need to produce lots of mosquito eggs.

So, those welts on your arm are a reminder that you've done your small part to help produce the next generation of healthy mosquitoes. But don't worry; days will start getting shorter in another month and winter will be back before we know it. And we will be back to sitting around the woodstove reminiscing about the summer—minus the bugs, of course.

It's been quite a summer here in Maine. Tourists and black flies came earlier and stayed longer than most years. Experts don't know if the habits of the flies and summer visitors are related, but if black flies could begin spending money like tourists they'd be a lot more welcome around these parts. And you can fit a lot more of them in smaller spaces.

With that in mind, grant writers and professors at our colleges and universities are no doubt beating the academic bushes looking for grant money to study the intriguing question of whether the habits of our native black flies and the habits of our summer visitors are, indeed, somehow related, and what exactly that might mean.

In other seasonal news, a spokesperson for the Yard, Flea and Garage Retailers Association (YFAGRA) said sales were off slightly in that important industry, which could have ripple effects (some would say a tidal wave effect) throughout Maine's economy, especially in the strategic dump sector—or "transfer station group," as the folks in Augusta insist we call it.

If the thousands of families in Maine's yard, flea and garage retail sector can't unload the piles and piles of "previously owned" items onto our summer visitors, and if those same summer visitors don't tie all that stuff onto their Volvo station

wagons and haul it back with them to Massachusetts and New Jersey, then those Maine families in the industry have to haul it to their dump (where they got it in the first place)—thus putting a strain on the state's disposal capacity. By season's end the state's economy has made less money from tourists and the industry must absorb the cost of rubbish disposal.

Sportsmen will be glad to hear that competition continues among the many motor home owners who clog Maine's traffic arteries each summer.

Motor home owners compete by coming to Maine in what they hope will be the longest and slowest motor home ever to visit the state. Once the true sportsmen among them acquire the longest motor home possible they often attach a large sport utility vehicle to the back and place a satellite dish on the top, just to make their vehicle longer, higher, and, most importantly, slower.

While in Maine, motor home competitors try other friendly sports like driving their block-long motor homes down some of our state's most congested roads at tortoise speed to see how many cars they can get stretched out behind them. The current record of 3,127 vehicles is held by a retired sausage manufacturer from Fond Du Lac, Wisconsin. The record was set on July 5 of this summer on a stretch of Route 1 between Wiscasset and Waldoboro. Two other favorite playing fields in these competitions include anywhere along Route 302, or Route 3 between Augusta and Belfast.

In other summer news, some folks tell me it wasn't such a good year for sport fishing, but reports say stories about fishing are still quite plentiful.

In closing, I'll tell you a fish story about the fella who was standing on a bridge fishing one of Maine's many fine rivers recently when a stranger came along and asked him how the fishing was.

"Pretty good, I'd say," said the fisherman. "As a matter of fact, in this very river on this very spot, I've caught a coupla dozen good size brook trout just this morning."

"Is that so," said the stranger. Pulling back his jacket to reveal a badge, the stranger said, "By the way, I think you should know that I'm the new game warden for this whole county."

"Is that so," said the fisherman, calmly. "In that case, I think you should know that I'm the biggest liar in the whole state of Maine."

Yes, it's March in Maine. And March means Mud Season.

One March morning recently, Nate Tuttle awoke at five, as was his custom. No matter whether it was winter or summer, Nate always got up at five. By six-thirty every morning he had fired up his old Queen Atlantic, made his coffee, gotten his paper, cooked and eaten his breakfast, cleaned up his dishes and was sitting in his front room by the big window in his favorite rocker just watching the road and finishing the crossword puzzle in the newspaper. He was a man of habit, and every morning it was the same routine.

So on this morning in March, Nate began his day as usual. After finishing his breakfast dishes, he came into the front room and took his seat. Gazing out the window, he noticed that down in front of the Pinkham place there was

a strange-looking furry black object just sitting there in the middle of the road.

"Now that's funny," Nate thought to himself. "I wonder what that is?"

He didn't think too much of it, and just kept working on his crossword puzzle.

A few hours later he looked up from his newspaper and noticed that the furry object had moved ever-so-slowly at least seventy-five feet closer to his own house, but it was still in the middle of the road and Nate still couldn't tell exactly what it was.

By mid-morning, he had also finished the word scramble and had read everything in the paper he intended to read, so he got up from his rocker to do a few chores around the house. Soon it was time for lunch.

Nate went into the kitchen, stoked up the fire and heated himself some beans and frankfurters. When the lunch dishes were all washed, Nate remembered the furry black object and walked into the front room to check on it.

Normally, Nate only went into his front room in the morning after breakfast, but he was so curious about that furry black object that he threw his routine to the March winds and walked right into that room, just as bold as brass.

By now the furry black object had pulled up in front of Nate's house, right there by the end of his front walk.

Nate put on his hat and coat and boots and walked to the end of his front walkway to get a closer look. When he got to the end of the walk, he got down on his hands and knees, reached out and grabbed the furry black object and lifted it up.

The strange object turned out to be just a furry winter hat. And, to his surprise, there under the furry winter hat Nate discovered Malcolm Martin, the postman.

"Pretty muddy walking, eh, Malcolm," Nate observed casually.

"Who's walking?" snapped Malcolm. "I'm riding my ATV!"

I saw a funny headline in a newspaper the other day: "Black flies due, despite cold spring."

I just had to smile.

Yes, I can understand why a newspaper would run an article about black flies. In the springtime, nothing will make a reader in these parts sit up and take notice and focus their attention faster than a newspaper headline that includes the two words: "black" and "flies."

It's just that I can't imagine the typical Maine resident sitting around the house on pins-and-needles wondering when some expert is going to tell us if there'll be any black flies around to hamper our gardening or ruin our cookouts this spring. Come to think of it, it's easier to imagine the typical Mainer choosing the pins-and-needles treatment over a backyard full of black flies—any day of the week.

Black flies are probably to Maine folks what those piranha fish are to the folks who live along the mighty Amazon River. Piranhas, for those who don't know, are those small, sharp-toothed fish that, according to the stories, travel in large, hostile groups and can devour an entire cow in seconds if they're hungry enough and if the cow is unfortunate enough to be in the wrong part of the Amazon River at the wrong time. Okay, so it's probably not a perfect comparison,

but a bunch of black flies can sure make life unpleasant in these parts for cows and people alike.

As a kid, I would sit and listen to horror stories about people getting caught out in the woods during black fly season and barely escaping with their lives.

My Uncle Abner used to tell about a trip he took upcountry years ago during black fly season when his car broke down.

"John," Uncle Abner would say, "when that car broke down, we were all just sitting there, trying to figure out what to do. It was black fly season and the black flies around the outside of the car were so thick we had to close all the car windows to keep the pesky things from getting inside. It was so cramped inside that car that soon we were having trouble breathing. Before long those black flies were all over the car windows so thick that it started getting dark inside that car and we could hardly see out."

I can't remember how Uncle Abner got out of that one, and I admit he might have been exaggerating a bit, only for emphasis. The point is this: It isn't hard to imagine something like that happening to anyone in Maine at this time of year.

Uncle Abner also insisted that black flies were first introduced into Maine as part of a state-sponsored tourist-control program that eventually went haywire. The idea was to place a bunch of these black flies here and there around the state in an effort to keep Maine from being overrun with pesky tourists. Fact is, we now have more black flies than ever. And they seem to be coming earlier and leaving later every year. Just like the tourists.

CHAPTER THREE

Local Color

The other day I was sitting at my fancy writer's desk, innocently reading one of the several newspapers I read each day, and I came across an article under the headline, "Heat's on to limit global warming." According to this article in *The Boston Globe*, an international panel of 2,000 scientists has concluded that the evidence is clear: global warming has already begun. And if you can't believe an international panel of 2,000 scientists, who can you believe? Except, maybe, the town gossip or the Board of Selectmen.

But after spending a fall season banking up the foundation, sealing up all the doors and windows, and getting snow tires and antifreeze; and after spending a long winter splitting and carrying almost five cords of firewood into the house, keeping the woodstove humming, and carrying out all the ashes, salting down the walkways and dodging plow trucks on the slippery roads when I drive to the store to buy head cold medicine—I have to admit that I don't get too upset when an international panel of 2,000 scientists tells me that it's getting a tad warmer outside.

Besides, I'm way ahead of that international panel of scientists, anyway. Back in the 1950s, my wise Uncle Abner tipped me off to this global warming business. And as far as I know, he never met an international scientist in his life.

A Moose and a Lobster Walk into a Bar . . .

As a kid, whenever it snowed and they called off school I'd walk down our road and visit my Uncle Abner. On one such visit I asked him to tell me all about the snowstorms when he was a boy back in the 1880s. That was all the encouragement he needed.

"When I was a boy," he'd begin, looking out the window at the swirling snow, "we had real snowstorms; not these flurries they call snowstorms these days."

I'd sit there wide-eyed as Uncle Abner told me about the blizzards of his childhood that raged for days, or even weeks.

"After a day or two of howling snow, we'd notice the small sheds would be buried first, and then the bigger out-buildings. As it continued to snow, whole houses would disappear, and people would have to dig themselves out of their attic windows. When the storm finally ended, you'd see some people walking around sticking poles into the snow, looking for their chimneys."

Uncle Abner also said it was much colder back in those days, too. "Cold?" he'd say. "I guess it was cold. One year the lake froze right to the bottom.

"In the bitter cold winter of 1885—the coldest ever recorded on this continent—the Gulf of Maine froze clear out to Monhegan," he said. "Steamboats from Boston couldn't come any closer to Maine than that ledge-of-an-island way out to sea."

Now, a scientist at the Massachusetts Institute of Technology—one of the members of the international panel of 2,000 scientists—says here in New England global warming could have severe repercussions.

But here in Maine, we've always had to deal with hard times. Uncle Abner used to say that the Great Depression wouldn't have been so bad if the times just before it hadn't been so hard.

If global warming gets serious here in Maine, we'll have to deal with it like Mainers have always dealt with difficult problems—try to look on the bright side or, more accurately, the "tad less dark side."

For example, this MIT scientist says global warming will lead to declines in the fall foliage season. That's the bad news. The good news is there'll be fewer "leaf peepers" coming up here in their Volvos, getting in the way and gawking at our trees. It just goes to show you what a few leafers will do to your disposition.

Global warming, the scientist says, will mean a reduction in forested land, which is bad. The good news is there'll be fewer people from Massachusetts sneaking up here to snitch a Christmas tree.

And as far as the prediction about the erosion of the coastline due to a rising sea level, that would be unfortunate. However, if I live long enough, my place here in South Paris might become prime, deep-water ocean frontage.

There are people in this world—and we always run into them when we least expect it—who always seem to be on the lookout for clues that people around them might be having a good time.

These grim, unpleasant people go around looking not just for the obvious signs of enjoyment in progress, but

for any hint that good times might break out somewhere. Happy people who are known to sing, laugh, dance or simply smile too much are just begging to be noticed and dealt with by these guardians. Parades, whether big or small, are also a good sign of merriment, and the people who march in them or enjoy watching them must eventually be dealt with. When these self-appointed, anti-amusement authorities spot any sort of good time—or if they even suspect that a certain group might be planning a good time—they move in swiftly to put a lid on it.

These serious-minded gendarmes against gladness can be found anywhere, and work under all kinds of assumed names and titles. They are easy to spot because they are gloomy and dour, and they belong to any number of serious-sounding organizations. One such brood is called PETA—People for the Ethical Treatment of Animals—sometimes called People Eating Tasty Animals by impertinent people who are obviously having too much fun.

I mention PETA because that particular glum group was in the news recently after it sent out a press release with the headline "PETA sets sights on Lobster Fest." The "fest" referred to is the annual Maine Lobster Festival in Rockland.

During each and every July since 1947, the good folks in the Knox County shire town of Rockland have gathered down by their waterfront for a lobster festival, a time for families and friends to celebrate the summer season with a tasty Maine lobster or two. Anyone who knows anything about Rockland knows that the lobster is a pretty important creature to the people in that area, as it is to lots of people all along the coast of Maine.

And so the people of Midcoast Maine take some time out of their busy summer lives and come together to enjoy a fine parade, some great entertainment and thousands of pounds of tasty steamed lobsters. In short—they have some fun.

Now, I admit, it took a while (about fifty years), but eventually PETA heard about all the fun and good times that folks were having at the Lobster Festival, and they made immediate plans to put an end to it.

The PETA folks would never come out and say they wanted to shut down Rockland's festival, but they launched what they called "a campaign to save lobsters from the boiling pot."

Without knowing much about these PETA people, I'd still be willing to bet that you could take everything this group knows about Maine lobsters, roll that information up into a ball, and fit every bit of it very neatly into the navel of a flea—and you'd still have room left over for six caraway seeds and an average lobster's brain.

Despite a considerable lack of knowledge, PETA came up to Maine and hired an airplane to fly over the festival carrying a giant banner with the message: "Being boiled hurts—Let Lobsters Live, Call 1-888-VEG-FOOD." Callers supposedly received a pack of veggie recipes that are probably as tasty as the boxes dealers use to ship those fresh lobsters around the world. The group also distributed 6,500 guilt-laden leaflets inside the *Bangor Daily News* explaining why animal protectionists are "steamed" about so many people obviously having so much fun at something the natives have the gall to call a Lobster Festival.

Based on nothing in particular, the PETA folks claim that lobsters have a sophisticated and not fully understood nervous system. Some crackpot scientist who supposedly studied lobsters somewhere "speculated" that these sea creatures are not able to go into shock, and thus they experience pain and suffering as they die.

In short, the PETA gang wants the good people of Rockland to feel all kinds of guilt and shame for all the fun and pleasure they've gotten at the expense of these sophisticated and innocent lobsters.

But don't get too worked up. Soon, word of other fun-seekers elsewhere will reach the PETA patrol and they'll be off once again to put an end to it. That's what they do.

After reading the PETA press release and giving it some serious thought, I have only one thing to say:

Pass the melted butter, please.

In the 1950s during snowy winter vacations my parents would pack up the station wagon and take us over to New Hampshire to go skiing. I remember for several winters we went to a family-owned inn called East Hill Farm in Jaffrey—right there in the shadow of Mount Monadnock. All the guests at East Hill Farm stayed right there in the owner's huge farmhouse and all our meals were served in the sprawling dining area.

There was a modest hill out back where all the trees had been cut down. The owner had put his Ford tractor at the foot of the hill, taken one of the back wheels off, attached a pulley to it and rigged up a rope-tow to haul his guests up the hill. It was a pretty basic operation, but we liked it. In those days, a ski vacation tended to be mostly a vacation. If you got a little skiing in around the edges that was fine, too.

Back then, skiing in these parts was definitely not what they now call a "mainstream" activity, and those who did ski tended to be a tad on the eccentric side—or else they were from northern Europe. At East Hill Farm back then, the best skiers by far weren't the hotshot college kids but were usually middle-aged guests with German-sounding accents—although because it was so soon after the war, they usually claimed to be "Swiss."

Once the sun went down there at East Hill Farm, there were no singles bars to hang out in or discos to go to. Everyone at the inn gathered around the huge fireplace in the front room and told stories or played Crazy Eights. That was the closest thing they had to a "night life" there in Jaffrey.

And you might not believe it to look at the place today, but back then North Conway was a quiet little village with a few family-owned clothing stores with quaint Alpine facades that made them look like they were high in the Alps. For that reason they sold things like Alpine sweaters, Alpine mittens, Alpine stocking hats and Alpine long johns.

I don't know exactly when it happened but at some point in the late fifties or early sixties the marketing crowd got a hold of skiing—and for some of us who remember the old days—it's been all downhill since then.

Soon after this serious marketing began it seemed everyone wanted to buy some equipment and head north to the ski slopes. The problem was there weren't that many ski slopes around these parts to head to. So, right here in quiet, staid, picturesque New England, big national corporations began buying up whole mountains and building massive ski resorts complete with restaurants, ski shops, night clubs and swimming pools, of all things. Before long the college crowd began skiing and on weekends in the winter all roads heading north were clogged with sports cars.

A Moose and a Lobster Walk into a Bar . . .

All these thoughts came back to me the other day when I picked up a newspaper and saw a banner headline declaring: "Study finds New England skiers growing older." I was a little surprised by the headline since I didn't find the the so-called news all that shocking. Would they prefer it if their skiers reached a certain age and then croaked, dying right out there on the slopes? Everyone on earth is older today than he or she was yesterday and—despite what we might spend on cosmetics or surgery—none of us is as young as we used to be. Why should skiers be any different?

According to the Longwoods International study—between 1994 and 1998—the average age of skiers in New England rose from 36.2 to 40.6, while the nationwide average rose more slowly from 37.6 to 38.7. That means that skiers here in New England got about four years older between 1994 and 1998. Now, I've never claimed to be a math whiz, but looking at those numbers, I'd say everyone alive at the time became at least four years older between 1994 and 1998, didn't they? Why should skiers be any different? That could just mean that skiers here in New England are healthier or less likely to go off the trail and run into a tree than skiers nationwide. And how do we know the other skiers in the nationwide study weren't lying about their ages?

The study was done for a group called the New England Ski Industry Summit. After hearing the results some members tried to laugh it off by making corny jokes and saying things like: "Oh no, the ski industry's over the hill." Others, who hadn't spent as much time in the lounge and were therefore more serious, said they were glad to hear that skiers here in New England were living longer and weren't dying off like they did in the old days.

Some said if the graying of the industry continues some changes will have to be made in the lodges and on the slopes.

They said you can look for early-bird discounts in the dining room, weekly Bingo and days when ladies with blue hair ski for half-price.

In most states, residents have a "thing" about out-of-staters in general. But there are folks from some other states who stand out in such numbers and tend to behave in such a manner that Maine residents bristle at the mere mention of that state. We're not mentioning any names, but if you've lived around here long enough, you can probably fill in the blanks yourself. (Hint: Just start with the letters Mass and go from there.)

Here in Maine, our "thing" with out-of-staters, or people "from away," is a big part of our history. From the beginning, Maine was sort of a buffer zone between the chunks of land claimed by the two European powers—England and France. Once the Brits defeated the French in the 1750s, the folks in Massachusetts somehow ended up controlling all of what is now Maine. At the time there weren't many people living here and the whole province was considered by Massachusetts folks to be little more than a giant woodlot— little more than trees and moose, which is very similar to how they really feel today. (Typical belief of Massachusetts summer visitors and the *Portland Press Herald* editors:

A Moose and a Lobster Walk into a Bar . . .

Maine is such a great state. If we can just get rid of all these unsightly and embarrassing locals . . .).

Anyway, every time folks in Maine wanted something they had to send someone, hat in hand, down to Boston to ask some Bay State official if it was okay.

Mainers couldn't even name their towns without getting the approval of the legislature down there in Massachusetts.

As you might expect, a thing like that can be aggravating and can sure get pretty old awfully fast. These days it's bad enough having to go up to Augusta to deal with the bureaucratic rascals up there—but at least they're *our* rascals. In politics, it's always easier dealing with your own homegrown rascals than those rascals from away.

Then in 1820—as part of the Missouri Compromise— the people of Maine managed to wrestle the land away from Massachusetts and set themselves up as an independent state. That arrangement worked just fine until about the 1970s. Then, for some reason (perhaps because they had already screwed up their own state), the people of Massachusetts decided they didn't like the 1820 deal at all and began buying back Maine one house lot at a time.

I agree that this thumbnail sketch of Maine history could be open to another interpretation by those sensitive folks who have different ideas and want to sketch things on their own thumbnail. To those individuals, we say: "Go back home!"

All seriousness aside, with the above information in mind, you can imagine my thoughts as I picked up a newspaper the other day and read two different articles about two different groups: One group wants to put a 3.2 million-acre national park right in the middle of things in northern Maine, and the other group has proposed reintroducing the gray wolf into the same area.

I guess the "one house lot at a time" plan is moving way too slow for the national park crowd. They figure, "let's just take it *all* back at once and be done with it." And to make sure no Mainer wanders around this national park of theirs, the other group wants it patrolled by roving packs of hungry gray wolves.

Unlike our early nineteenth-century arrangement with people from away, this 3.2 million-acre chunk of land patrolled by wolves wouldn't be controlled by bureaucrats in Massachusetts. No; being a national park, it would, of course, be controlled by national bureaucrats in Washington, D.C.

As you might expect, people up north who have been using this same 3.2 million acres for such frivolous things as earning a living, raising families, and living their lives, aren't too amused or even pleased with this new out-of-state idea. Even Governor Angus King doesn't seem to be too impressed with the national park plan.

He said, "People have to understand the implications of the word 'national.' What we're talking about here is ownership, management and control of 15 percent of the state of Maine in Washington, D.C.—not our own elected officials, or anyone accountable to you or me, but by the federal bureaucracy."

Like the rest of us, the governor and the folks up north know how much fun it can be to get something approved by a board of selectmen or a planning board. We have no desire to deal, any more than necessary, with folks in Washington, most of whom think Maine should be—or already is—part of Canada, anyway.

It's also not too shocking to learn that the idea of reintroducing gray wolves into northern Maine is being met with the same skepticism and opposition.

A Moose and a Lobster Walk into a Bar . . .

Darren Giles, a resident of the north country, told a reporter that he has seen what coyotes can do to deer, livestock and pets, and he thinks reintroducing wolves is crazy. He believes the whole idea is being pushed by what he calls "out-of-state elitists" who have no clue as to what Maine is about. What's more, he doesn't think the gray wolf supporters—Defenders of Wildlife—have been forthcoming with information about the consequences of reintroduction.

So here we are, 180 years after wrestling control of Maine from the folks in Massachusetts and becoming an independent state, having to wrestle with folks who are doing everything they can to take over Maine, again.

Time to call up the militia, I guess.

I'm fully prepared right here and now to open a can of worms and discuss a topic that I think has been ignored for too long. But before I do that, and to show how serious I am about all this, I want to lift a brief excerpt from the Constitution of the State of Maine. Article I, Section 1 says: "All people . . . have certain natural, inherent and unalienable rights, among which are those of . . . possessing and protecting property . . ."

That's right. A Mainer's right to private property. How's your private property doing these days?

It wasn't too long ago here in Maine that you didn't have to worry about protecting your private property, even in tourist season. And that was just fine. That was the way everyone liked it.

I knew people upcountry who never locked their houses or cars. An uncle of mine once had to call a locksmith to put locks on the doors to his house—not because he didn't feel safe, but because he was selling the house and the real estate agent said he would have to give the new owner a house key at the closing.

"That house doesn't have a key," my uncle said. "Never had a key to that place, because we never felt a need to lock it."

"Well, you better get yourself a house key pretty darn quick, that's all I can say," said the agent, "because the people buying it are from away and you can bet they'll want to be locking it."

Another fella from back home, Thurland Beal, once had his pickup stolen from the front of the old Red & White. Thurland had gone into the store to buy a few items and swap some gossip, and when he came back out, his truck was gone. First, he thought the truck's brakes had slipped and the truck had rolled itself to a lower part of town. After looking all over, he finally had to admit that his truck had been stolen.

When Eldridge Seavey, the local deputy, was taking the report, he asked Thurland if perhaps he had left his keys in the truck. Thurland couldn't believe this silly question. He snapped, "Darn right the keys were in the truck. Where else would I keep them? I haven't taken the keys out of that truck since I drove it home from the dealer years ago." To Thurland, it shouldn't have made a bit of a difference that the keys were in the truck. In Maine, you just didn't take what wasn't yours.

Over the years, things sure have changed here in Maine, even back home. These days in the fall, the people who own

stands of Christmas trees now have to guard those trees night and day from the few dishonest people among us who like to observe Christmas by cutting down a truckload of someone else's trees and hauling them to a parking lot somewhere else to sell. Some of the people who make Christmas wreaths have occasionally preyed on wood lot owners for evergreen tips and boughs. It got so bad upcountry that a law had to be passed in Augusta saying you needed an official certificate from the state that showed you had the wood lot owner's permission to cut before you began hauling a truckload of tips and boughs out of the woods.

Now, just to prove that nothing around here is safe anymore unless it's nailed down, there are some dishonest rascals among us running around stealing some of Maine's most beautiful perennials—day lilies and lupine.

As I've traveled around the state this spring telling my stories, people have told me their own horror stories of the growing problem with flower desperados who ride around in station wagons preying on innocent beds of lupines and lilies. Try and imagine it: middle-class couples in late-model wagons with nothing better to do than ride around looking for flowers to steal. They stop along the side of a road, get out, run up an embankment and start ripping up thick clumps of lupine. Then they throw the ill-gotten perennials into the back of their wagon and flee.

You have to ask yourself: What is going on around here when lilies and lupine aren't safe? And just what is the gang up there in the Legislature planning to do about it?

There was an item in the newspaper the other day that caught my eye. It told of a company from Korea that is now buying four thousand pounds of whelks a week here in Maine, processing them and shipping them back to Korea. But the story didn't end there. It went on to say that these folks from Korea eventually want to import between 20,000 and 40,000 pounds of whelks a day.

For those who don't know, a whelk is like what we used to call a periwinkle; a snail-like critter that lives in the ocean. Nobody around these parts ever had much use for whelks because no one knew what to do with them. Now these folks from Korea are willing to pay good money for Maine whelks, and then ship them back to Korea. Kinda makes you wonder what else we have laying around here that we don't have any particular use for but could sell for, cash in the global marketplace.

That, by the way, is how our native yard sale got going here in Maine—with the idea that your worthless stuff might be quite valuable to somebody somewhere else. All you had to do was haul it out onto your lawn and see if someone came along and showed any interest in it.

Anyway, in case you haven't looked at a calendar recently, we're about to enter Maine's most vibrant and important money-making season—yard sale season.

And as a public service to our friends from Korea, I thought I'd give a little background on our yard sale industry in case they might want to check them out while they're waiting for their Maine whelks to be processed.

During the warm weather spell we have for a few weeks every year, yard sales play a major part in our state's economy. You probably know from your research that tourists and lobsters are also pretty important here in Maine. But

for sheer volume and gross sales (and you should be warned that, like whelks, some yard sales can be pretty gross)—nothing can touch our homegrown Maine yard sales.

Speaking of sales, I'd also be willing to bet that there are state tax collectors at our capital in Augusta who can't sleep nights, who toss and turn in their feather beds, disturbed by the whole idea of yard sales. Why? It's not all the fine items being sold off countless lawns all over the state that upset the tax collectors. It's the fact that sales are being made without the benefit of a regulation or sales tax.

Crude attempts have been made around here over the years by some political entities to collect money for yard sales. Some towns and cities now require permits and the like. But the vast majority of our yard sales go humming along wide open and completely unregulated and untaxed. And it's enough to give our homegrown tax collectors a peptic ulcer.

If you spend any time here in Maine driving around looking for yard sales you'll soon discover certain things. The best yard sales are in front of large old country homes on tree-shaded streets. A yard sale in front of a small ranch house might appear to have a lot of stuff, but it's usually a clever optical illusion. You might stand in awe and wonder how all that clothing and furniture on the lawn could have come from such a little house or trailer. But such sales are never much good. That's because the folks in the trailer or ranch had their best yard sale when they sold off several tons of family treasures so they could move into the small house or trailer in the first place.

You should also know that many people in Maine have permanent yard sales on their lawns that will run from about June right through Labor Day. To keep these long-running yard sales stocked, these people will go around and buy up stuff from other yard sales, mark them up a bit, and put them on their own lawn. This is also known as Down East recycling. An item can start off the season on a lawn in Bethel and end up the season on a lawn in Boothbay. Some day it may start off in Kennebunk and end up in Corea.

Anyway, now that Maine whelks have become an item of international trade, I think it's only a matter of time before the venerable yard sale goes international. And as host of the popular WGAN Tag Sale—a yard sale on the air—I'd like to offer myself as a trade representative to places like Korea the next time the governor puts a committee together to talk trade abroad.

If folks are willing to come all the way from Korea to buy what we used to think of as worthless whelks—why wouldn't they be interested in our old kitchen sets, dishes and unused wedding gifts?

As a kid back home I used to read those popular national magazines like *Life* and *Look* and learn all about the latest fads that were sweeping the country in the fifties and sixties—like hula hoops, coonskin caps, Mexican food and lawn ornaments. Then I'd sit and wonder to myself how long it would take one fad or another to make it up here to Maine and, particularly, to my town.

Sometimes, a big national fad would only take a year or two to catch on here in Maine; sometimes, it would take a full five years or more. And sometimes, a fad would never come at all. It would get about as far as the traffic circle in Portsmouth and just die out right there in the middle of the street.

Even if a national fad did make it up here to Maine, it would often be modified for our own particular purposes. For example, knowing that the hula hoop fad wouldn't last too long, most folks here in Maine didn't want to waste money buying a fancy one at an expensive store. Most Mainers figured it was easy enough to make their own hula hoops for the kids out of an old garden hose. And I knew a kid who had a "modified" Down East-style coonskin cap that his father made out of an old fishing cap and a squirrel tail. Although, as far as lawn ornaments go there's not enough room here to go over all the contributions of Mainers to that field of endeavor.

It now looks as though Southern California—which went way over its fad quota a long time ago, as far as I'm concerned—is about to hatch another foolish craze.

According to an Associated Press story, plans are in the works there in trendy Southern California for "oxygen bars"—places where patrons will be able to relax and inhale twenty-minute doses of oxygen for about sixteen dollars.

Proponents say recreational oxygen blasts (plain or fruit-scented) can ease headaches, boost alertness, fight fatigue and reduce stress. One entrepreneur plans to open two bars this fall that will feature $70 oxygen facials and $125 oxygen body wraps.

Now, I have no idea if this crazy California fad of oxygen bars will ever make it to Maine; but if it does, I can guarantee you some Mainer will tinker with it and improve it with a few simple Down East adjustments. I just might try to take advantage of this idea myself.

I'm pretty sure that if these oxygen bars ever pop up here in Maine, they'd probably show up first in Portland's trendy Old Port section. The crowd that runs those Old Port shops seems to be good at making lots of money selling lots of things that most of us wouldn't even think of buying or admit to owning. All those well-to-do people in Southern Maine (who have so much more money than they know what to do with) like to go to those Old Port shops to unload some of the extra cash in their wallets that's been weighing them down. And those Old Port shop owners are always more than willing to help them unload that excess weight.

But some of the rich folks who visit the Old Port are former poor folks from Maine's poorer counties. And that's where I think this oxygen bar idea can be modified for Maine purposes.

Around Portland over the years, I've heard lots of people—originally from the western foothills of the County or from way Down East—talk about how they miss their hometowns and how if they could've earned a living back there, they never would have left.

I'm not a gambling man, but I'd be willing to bet these lost souls would appreciate a bar modeled after these oxygen bars in California. They could go not for whiffs of pure oxygen, but instead to inhale from canisters that contained air from the small hometowns they left behind.

Someone from Down East would take a whiff from a canister filled with air that smelled just like the fish-packing plants and clam flats of home. Others from Rumford or Jay would take a whiff from another canister and be reminded of the nostalgic aroma of the paper mills back in their hometowns. Folks raised on farms could pay a certain amount and for twenty minutes they could inhale the scent of barns and

cow pastures. One whiff and whoosh—they'd be home—if only for a while.

There's no end to the possibilities. Special effects like mosquitoes and black flies could also be added.

The motto for such a business might be: "No matter what the smell, there's no place like home."

Experts who claim to know about such things often say that "Politics makes strange bedfellows." The saying has something to do with how people who disagree on just about everything else occasionally end up "in bed," or on the same side, of some hot political issue. A recent example of this old maxim was the odd alliance of sorts between radical environmentalist Jonathan Carter and conservative operative Mary Adams. I can tell without even asking that these two people have never agreed on much, but they managed to do their part to help defeat the proposed forest compact. And in doing so, Adams and Carter tripped up Governor Angus King, the man who has been the most popular governor in America.

It occurred to me as I watched the election returns on television that Carter and Adams were a lot like people I knew back in the 1970s.

Back home years ago, someone like Jonathan Carter would have been known around town as a "hippie," and Mary Adams would have been known as a "local."

It's been almost thirty years now since the first wave of back-to-the-land hippies like Carter started arriving here in Maine in great numbers—buying old farms in small towns all over the state and causing quite a stir among the locals. (To see a real 1970s-style hippie today, visit the Common Ground Fair some fall.)

In those days our town locals would drive around in a good reliable American car like a Ford or Chevy. Hippies tended to drive foreign, funny-looking things like Volvos and Saabs. By driving such odd-looking vehicles those early hippies were pretty easy to spot.

Locals in those days shopped at places like the Red & White and Reny's and always read the local paper. Local stores were filled with essentials like white bread, red hot dogs and beer. The local paper was filled with important news about things like your high school basketball scores and the weekly menu at the school.

Hippies tended to shop out of the Whole Earth catalogs or frequent the fledgling health food stores, where you would never find red hot dogs or Narragansett beer. They avoided the local paper and would go through quite a bit of trouble to get a paper from away like the hippie/liberal-slant-ed *Boston Globe* or *The New York Times*. Those papers from away never carried anything the regular folks in town wanted to read. If hippies read any local paper it was the *Maine Times*, which always made a point of never carrying basketball scores or school menus.

Like Jonathan and Mary, hippies and locals in those days didn't agree on much. When locals sprayed their blueberry fields, hippies protested and tried to convince the locals to use organic methods of growing blueberries or controlling insects. When hippies posted their land against hunting or

spraying, locals protested and said the hippies knew nothing about life in rural Maine.

Locals had their organizations like snowmobile clubs and Odd Fellows and the hippies had their organizations, too, like "free schools" and food co-ops—which always sounded a tad too socialist for many locals. Locals liked nothing better than a weekend of snowmobiling, and loved hot, smoke-filled bingo halls and the roar of a chain saw or dirt bike. Hippies spent their time contra dancing and cross-country skiing, and enjoyed the peace and quiet of hiking.

The kids of locals had good Maine names like Perley and Clayton. Hippie kids tended to have names like Karma and Eagle Feather.

Locals and hippies would come together and get a good look at each other at the post office or school board meetings, and at the annual town meeting. On those occasions the locals would sit and roll their eyes when some hippie would take the floor and go off about some nonsensical idea or another. Since the locals outnumbered the hippies by quite a margin, the nonsensical idea was usually voted down in short order.

Years ago I had a neighbor who often used the word "hippie" to describe very different people in town—people who didn't appear to have much in common. Confused at her use of the word "hippie," I once asked her, "Theo, what is a hippie?"

She looked at me a little quizzically, thinking that I, of all people, should know things like what a hippie is. After thinking it over for a minute she said:

"Well, I'd say a hippie is someone who comes here from away, lives here even though they don't have to, and talks funny."

Nowadays, a whole generation of kids that were born to those 1970s hippies and raised right here in Maine are becoming parents themselves. Some of those hippies even assume that their children and grandchildren are finally considered Maine natives.

But like an old Mainer once said to his neighbor from away who wondered if his kids were considered Maine natives since they were born right here:

"Well, if my cat had kittens in the oven, I wouldn't call them biscuits."

Probably not, and I don't think he'd call them Eagle Feather, either.

Someone once said, "You can tell a lot about a people by seeing what they choose to collect in their museums, and what they choose to dispose of in their dumps."

Along those lines, a clever individual back home used to say, "If it weren't for the town dump, we'd have almost nothing to argue about around here."

I bring up the whole delicate subject of dumps because I recently saw an article in the newspaper about how Portland's Regional Waste System folks are going to start charging commercial dumpers $25 per ton for the privilege of disposing of their prime rubbish. The fee is supposed to help the city cover a $1 million increase in the cost of incinerating its trash. Here in Maine, the cost of disposing of our once-useful rubbish keeps getting higher and higher.

A Moose and a Lobster Walk into a Bar . . .

And it didn't used to be like that. After reading the article, I thought of how complex and sophisticated the whole business of trash has become. I began to wonder if, in these final years of the twentieth century, we had advanced at all in the field of rubbish and trash handling.

Not having enough formal places like museums to pile old things in, here in Maine we've improvised and developed things like sprawling farmhouses and double-wide trailers. Folks in these large houses and trailers seldom need the extra living space. What they always need is more collecting space. And when their houses and trailers are filled, they pile things outside in their dooryard. I don't have to know the particulars to know that the cluttered dooryard was developed by an inspired Down Easter who was just pressed for storage space.

Long before bureaucrats came up with "transfer stations"— where trash is assembled before it's transferred to giant, centrally located, federally funded incinerators—we here in Maine had other more useful options. Folks in small Maine towns had what were affectionately called town dumps.

Whenever I think of dumps, I'm reminded of my friend Lincoln Peavey. Lincoln would load up his pickup with a week's worth of trash and haul it to the town dump. Once he threw everything out of the truck and over the bank, Lincoln would jump off his pickup and carefully survey the dump's unique and ever-changing horizon.

On a good day, he'd eventually see something like an old washing machine or an outboard motor carelessly thrown on the dump. He knew those machines only needed a little tinkering, so Lincoln would throw those treasures onto his pickup. Then he might see an old wooden door and realize it was just the kind of door he'd need in his hunting camp, once he and his brother Eldridge got around to framing-out the camp.

He'd go on like that most of the morning with one thing after another, until he'd eventually have a lot more stuff balanced on that pickup of his than he hauled to the dump in the first place. Once that truck was filled, he'd "transfer" all that useful stuff to his dooryard.

Recalling the newspaper article about Portland's troubles with dumping, it occurred to me that back home we didn't start to have rumblings in the town's rubbish circles until our selectmen returned from a national rubbish symposium in Las Vegas. They say all the big names in rubbish were there making fancy speeches about new fads and trends in the field of rubbish. When those starry-eyed selectmen got home—their heads now filled with rubbish—they couldn't wait to pass an ordinance against such revered Maine customs as dump picking and other traditional recycling techniques.

Once that "No Dump Picking" ordinance was passed and strictly enforced, it was all downhill at the town dump. You see, when dump-pickers like Lincoln Peavey were not allowed to remove truckloads of rubbish, huge mounds of the stuff began to overwhelm our town dump. Eventually it had to be closed, and modern transfer stations replaced them.

Sometimes, when I take the rubbish to the transfer station, I miss Lincoln Peavey and the old town dump.

A Moose and a Lobster Walk into a Bar . . .

There are a few things that people from out-of-state find curious about Maine. One of them is the soft drink known as Moxie and its connection to Maine history.

According to experts, the closest thing to soft drinks in the 1800s, when Moxie first appeared, was "impregnated water" (don't look at me), a corked bottle of carbonated water that was prepared and peddled in various localities as "health tonic."

Moxie was the first mass-marketed soft drink in our country, arriving on the scene long before Pepsi or Coca-Cola.

One Moxie story claims that after the Civil War, a Lieutenant Moxie went down to the vast unexplored jungles of South America and, while poking around near the Straits of Magellan, discovered a starchy plant known to the locals to have great powers, giving "durable and vigorous feelings." This same Lieutenant Moxie returned to the United States and used the magical plant as the main ingredient in his new health tonic—Moxie.

Great story, but no one has ever documented that anyone named Lieutenant Moxie fought, or even prepared meals, for either side in our Civil War. Besides that, no scientific reference has ever been published on any South American starchy plant that supposedly had medicinal properties.

So much for that particular Moxie legend. But, if it is not to your liking, don't worry. Over the last century, the Moxie people have unearthed many stories about the product's origin.

Typical of all tonics of the age, the makers of Moxie claimed that its product could cure almost anything, including paralysis, nervous exhaustion, softening of the brain, insanity, and what people delicately referred to as "loss of manhood." As a nostrum, or tonic, or quack medicine, Moxie was originally dispensed a spoonful at a time. It was first marketed as a patent medicine in Lowell, Massachusetts around 1876.

But Moxie does have a Maine connection. In 1884, Dr. Augustin Thompson of Union changed Moxie to take advantage of the new and growing soft drink market. The tonic became known as "Beverage Moxie—Nerve Food." Later, that was shortened to: "Moxie:—that awful tasting stuff," or something like that.

From the turn of the century until the 1920s, Moxie was America's most popular soft drink. It was President Calvin Coolidge's favorite beverage.

As far as I'm concerned, Moxie's biggest problem is that it tastes just like crankcase oil that's been in the crankcase for 50,000 miles. They say it was originally very bitter and medicinal-tasting, but I can't imagine anything tasting worse than today's Moxie. The primary ingredient is said to be extract of gentian root. Another ingredient is wintergreen, an herb that was known as "moxie" when the formula was first concocted. Other claims to the name Moxie come from our state's Moxie Falls, Moxie Cave, Moxie Pond, Moxie Stream, Moxie Lake, East Moxie Township, Moxie Gore, moxie berries and moxie plums.

A recipe book lists Moxie's main ingredients as oats, sassafras and wintergreen. A later label lists water, sugar, cinchona (a bitter South American bark), alkaloids, caramel, and flavoring. Many early quack medicines, including the original Coca-Cola formula, had cocaine as a beneficial. Some speculate that Moxie also once included cocaine to cure nervous exhaustion and that "loss of manhood" condition. In 1906, the Food and Drug Act outlawed cocaine. The formula then changed.

In the 1960s, the FDA ruled that sassafras may cause cancer, and outlawed its use in food. So, Moxie changed its formula again.

A Moose and a Lobster Walk into a Bar . . .

Today, it's said that Moxie is flavored primarily with extracts of gentian root and wintergreen. Although it lacks sassafras, experts say Moxie tastes pretty much the way it did in the good old days.

Mark your calendars now, because every year on the second Saturday in July, upwards of 30,000 Moxie fans descend on the little village of Lisbon Falls for the annual Moxie Day Festival.

The Moxie Day Festival has drawn crowds from around the country. The sidewalks turn orange with Moxie shirts, and even the dogs are dressed up in orange bandannas.

The festival is the brainchild of Moxie-lover Frank Anicetti, owner of the Kennebec Fruit store in Lisbon Falls. Frank sells Moxie in his store—as well as candy, ice cream, T-shirts, caps, posters and all sorts of other merchandise extolling Moxie. He even claims to be "A Moxie Drinker."

I might claim that someday, too, but it will never be true. Pass the crankcase oil, please.

One important thing to remember about Maine is that fall is fair season and there should always be a fair going on at a fairgrounds near you. And no matter how hectic your life is, you shouldn't let fair season pass without going to at least one of Maine's many county fairs.

Why? Well, as health nuts already know, fried dough, the official food of all Maine fairs, contains lots of those two critical dietary staples—fat and sugar. And the average fairgoer eats about five pounds of fried dough per visit. So, right off, fairs are good for you.

My local fair is the Oxford County Fair, which brings us to an important rule of county fairs: If you're going to go to a fair (and you really should), you should attend the one that's closest to your town. It really should be a law. As a kid in Washington County, I remember our fair moved several times over the years—from the western part of the county to farther east, and eventually back again to the west.

I also remember that some of the fiercest arguments I ever saw adults get into were not about schools or taxes or Vietnam. Instead, selectmen's meetings would last into the wee hours of the morning while people argued about the fair. Families would break up, and friendships would be destroyed—all over the question of where to put that fair.

It was said political careers were made or destroyed on the issue of the fair. Folks didn't care about a politician's race, religion, creed, place of origin (as long as it wasn't Bangor), political affiliation—whatever. Folks didn't even care if the politician was divorced or running around. A candidate for local office could even be a Democrat as long as he or she held the right views on the Washington County Fair.

If you don't think a fair's location is still an important issue, try this little experiment. Sit down and write a letter to the local newspaper saying why you think they should move the local fair from its present location to some place up the road about ten to twenty miles. Next, get about a dozen friends to do the same thing. Then, just sit back and see what happens.

Have fun writing, and see you at the fair!

A Moose and a Lobster Walk into a Bar . . .

I travel around our beautiful state a lot on important sto-rytelling missions and other flimsy assignments. While driving along Maine's roads you can't help but be impressed by the thought and effort and bizarre creativity that some folks obviously put into decorating their mailboxes and mail-box posts. Mailbox art has been ignored by the haughty art critics in the state (all located in the Massachusetts suburb of Portland, I might add), but a lot of roadside art is pretty "artistic," and has provided me and other drivers with a lot of . . . well, I can't really say exactly what it's provided us with, but I know it's sure provided us with a lot of it.

How often have you been riding along some country road and come around a curve and all of a sudden you're staring at a construction of some kind by the side of the road that can only be described as a tad strange. Often, you're not quite sure what it is, or are too embarrassed to admit even to yourself that you might know what it is. (According to the experts, that's what makes something "real art"—strange and unidentifiable.)

On some occasions, I have pulled over to the side of the road, stared for a while, and then asked myself: "What kind of person do you suppose would think up such an odd idea for a mailbox?" And then I wonder: "What kind of person do you suppose would put such an odd creation out here by the side of the road for everyone to gawk at?"

Over the years I've driven by mailboxes that in one way or another involved such things as water pumps, engine blocks, power tools, furniture, fish nets, lobster traps, animal traps, representations of livestock, poultry, produce, mannequins, boats, cars, trucks, planes, farm implements, outhouses, various species of fish and game, spacecraft, cartoon characters, famous people, and other items I don't even dare to mention in polite company.

There was a restaurant Down East that had a mailbox shaped like an oven, a bait dealer who had one shaped like a miniature bait barrel, and a plumber who had one shaped like a . . . well, you get the idea.

One of my favorite pieces of mailbox art was a mailbox for a family-run ice cream business. The large mailbox was set in what was supposed to be a giant scoop of ice cream, painted a pale, sickly green, on top of a brown cone. I can only guess that it was supposed to be pistachio ice cream. To get to the mailbox itself you had to lift up the scoop of ice cream.

Alongside the ice cream was a large red ball that I'm only guessing was supposed to be a giant maraschino cherry. The red ball was on an iron rod and could be raised to indicate that there were items inside the mailbox to be picked up.

There was a mailbox artist in our town who was so disgusted with having his artwork whacked by the town snowplow several times each winter that he came up with a post that could have withstood a direct hit from a good-sized artillery shell. His post hole went into the ground almost eight feet, and the post itself was a steel pipe filled with reinforced concrete. After some plow trucks bounced off it a few times the drivers started giving it a wide berth. Eventually they decided to stop plowing his road altogether. He passed on a few years back, but that post of his is still standing there as a fitting memorial.

A Moose and a Lobster Walk into a Bar . . .

Despite its shortcomings, the U.S. Postal Service is almost as broadminded as the National Endowment for the Arts gang when it comes to what it will allow for artistic expression in the area of mailboxes. In general, if your mailbox is set a "reasonable distance" from the road, is between 36 inches and 42 inches high, and has a tight door (to keep that junk mail nice and dry), the post office will allow it.

As I drove by a particularly garish piece of mailbox art the other day, I got to thinking about a possible compromise solution to the debate over government funding for the arts.

Never mind the arty types in Washington or New York. Why not let the U.S. Postal Service give out grants for original mailbox art? It would go a long way toward encouraging what the art critics like to call—"an authentic indigenous art form."

CHAPTER FOUR

Of the People, For the People

I'm told that soon after the first settlers arrived in this part of the world, they began planning for an odd assembly that eventually became known as the town meeting. After a period of trial and error, March was picked as the perfect time of year to hold these meetings. It is unquestionably the most useless stretch of thirty-one days on the calendar.

What else is there for decent, hardworking citizens in Maine to do in March but sit around a drab town hall for a few hours and argue with neighbors about the town's problems? Even folks in those rare towns that don't have any problems can easily imagine they have them in March, when the weather has a way of making everything around these parts seem worse than it really is.

Conspiracy-types back home used to say that road commissioners cleverly arranged for March town meetings. They argued that no one in their right mind would vote against a town's road budget—no matter how high—after riding over those same roads to get to a town meeting in March.

Okay. The cynical among you are surely saying, "Anyone in their right mind makes plans to be quite a bit south of Maine come March."

Good point.

Anyway, some of our trendier Maine towns—those with no respect for history and New England traditions—have abandoned their March meeting like some rusty old car, and have decided to have their town meetings in months like May or June or, worst of all, August.

But experts (that's any regular customer at your town's favorite morning coffee spot) know that March is the best month for these unique gatherings. In March, we're less likely to be bothered by things like pesky out-of-state visitors. Who else would you find in Maine in March except those of us who have to be here?

Folks back in the old days knew you couldn't work in the woods in March because of mud season, and, for the same reason, you couldn't do much in the fields, either. So they decided to come together in March and get all the town's unpleasant business out of the way before nice weather arrived.

Good town meetings have skilled moderators who keep things moving right along. But there's always some little warrant article that will bring the whole darn meeting to a grinding halt. It usually involves some nonprofit group or agency looking for a few hundred dollars from the town. The same townspeople who just raised their hands to approve spending a few hundred thousand dollars for roads and equipment will develop a kind of paralysis when it comes to approving a few hundred dollars for the agency.

Back home when I was a kid, the town manager who always planned our town's March meetings was Amos Smith. At selectmen's meetings, when asked something like, "How many people work for the town now, Amos?" He would scratch his head and say something like, "Hardly any of them."

I heard recently that Amos finally retired after managing the building of a new town hall that they plan to name after him. Selectmen hired a new town manager from away, Fred

Clark, who says he plans to tear up the pea patch there in town and finally get some things done.

Folks say Fred is one of those fellas who imagines he's more important than he really is. His first day on the job, he came into that new town hall and got right to work planning for the next town meeting.

A fella came into Fred's office and Fred just had to impress him with how important he was. So, as the fella waited, Fred picked up his fancy telephone and just sat there pretending to talk important town business.

When he thought the poor fella was duly impressed, Fred said "Good-bye," and put the phone down. Then he turned to the fella and said, "Yes, sir, I think I have a minute to spare between phone calls. Can I help you with something?"

The fella grinned a bit and said, "Yes. I'm here to hook up your new telephone."

While the rest of us in Maine stumble awkwardly through our workdays trying to get by, our public servants in the legislature adroitly wrangle over the important issues that will ultimately affect our very lives, shape our futures and our fortunes, and, apparently even determine our dancing shoes.

According to recent newspaper articles, a recent legislative brawl has erupted over the issue of "the dance." You might not be aware of this, but ever since Maine has been a certified dues-paying member of these United States, we have been operating our fine state without an official State of Maine dance. Kinda makes you weak in the knees just thinking about it.

Everyone knows how upset law enforcement folks get when they catch someone operating a motor vehicle without an official driver's license properly issued by our Motor Vehicle Department. And just try building a house on your lot without an official building permit. Yet our state officials, the very people we depend on to look after our vital interests, apparently see nothing wrong with operating our great state without something as critical as an official state dance.

For many years now, the people of Maine have been going about their daily business under the false impression that urgent questions like the official state tree (white pine), the official state cat (Maine coon), the official mineral (tourmaline) and the official state dance had been dealt with and were behind us. Fact is, no such resolution has ever been reached on the latter issue.

Now, with all the skill our public officials exhibit when waltzing around one tough issue and sidestepping another, you'd think an official State of Maine dance would be a pretty easy assignment for them. But it isn't. Not only have we been operating our state without an official state dance all these years, our two-stepping legislators and tap-dancing governor can't agree even at this late date on what steps to take to determine what our official state dance should be.

A recent news article said that a bill to designate square dancing as the official state dance is still sitting on Governor Angus King's desk while he tries to nimbly sidestep the whole issue. And a move is now afoot, led by the gang at the Arts Commission, to have the already clogged legislature reconsider the whole contentious dance issue one more time.

Some critics (and when it comes to something as indispensable as an official state dance, everyone, it appears, is now a critic) have complained that the measure ignores the cultural diversity in Maine by singling out one form of dance. The governor has been urged by the arty crowd to veto the measure even though it passed in the House and Senate.

The only question I have is: Where were these culturally diverse hoofers when the legislature was considering this crucial piece of legislation in the first place? Every dance aficionado in the state—anyone who is anyone in the dance community—apparently knew about this critical measure, and they were supposed to see to it that their well-heeled members were in Augusta to help choreograph the official dance hearings.

Legislative watchers said they'd never seen anything like it before. On the day the official dance bill had its unveiling, the hallowed halls of the Capitol became dance halls for a day. Its stately corridors echoed to the sounds of tap shoes, the clomping from thousands of cloggers was deafening, and the hearing room itself at one point was wall-to-wall tutus.

Dance lobbyists were everywhere, buttonholing swing votes among the legislators and trying to sway them with offers of free tap lessons, or the opportunity to be a celebrity caller at a square dance in some key legislative district during the next election.

But now, they say, the governor wants to take it from the top, and a lawmaker from upcountry wants the legislature to recall the bill and do-si-do back to the hearing room to consider what steps to take now.

When a political pundit said a vote to reconsider the square dance bill would be "difficult to call," a critic from the

Arts Commission said such "exclusionary language" should be avoided when discussing something as touchy as dancing.

Meanwhile, the State of Maine limps along without an official state dance and square dancers from across the country are threatening massive promenades in protest.

Our pastor back home would often begin his Sunday sermons with a quote like: "The road to hell is paved with good intentions." Local critics of our town government

would often use the occasion of such remarks to mumble under their breath something like: "At least those roads get paved."

Two recent newspaper articles made me think of old Pastor Woodward and his saying about good intentions. One article was about the plan by the Department of Transportation (a gang that surely knows something about paving and roads) to put signs out on the Maine Turnpike warning motorists that they can expect long delays if they dare venture off the turnpike and take Route 1 up the coast. The other was about the state being in the liquor business.

Concerning the DOT plan, a lot of business owners on Route 1 don't want all those unsuspecting tourists to have any information about traffic conditions. You really cannot blame them. If I owned a thriving tourist business over there on the coast, do you think I'd want those thousands and thousands of rich out-of-staters to know that they're headed for the longest and most tangled traffic mess anywhere in Maine? I don't think so.

The DOT says all they want to do is help relieve some of that notorious coastal traffic congestion. A good intention if I ever heard one.

But local business owners along the coast will hear none of it. The owners of tourist businesses say the rich tourists from places like Massachusetts and New Jersey tolerate and even expect traffic delays. And if the highway gang makes an issue of it, those tourists will just go elsewhere. I don't know how those business owners know all that about tourists. I guess they just do.

Then after thinking about it for a while, I decided that those business owners might be looking further down the road—so to speak—and are concerned with something else entirely. Follow me.

What if the DOT follows through on its good intentions and puts up these helpful, informative signs telling tourists about traffic delays? What then? Well, suppose our summer visitors decide they don't like long, slow-moving lines of traffic and they like having the DOT provide such information. And suppose further that tourists start asking for more informational signs. Those business owners know already that such a trend could be dangerous, and there's just no telling where such a path might lead.

Someday the folks at the DOT might get completely out of control and start posting signs that read: "Tacky gift shops with shoddy merchandise just ahead," or "Expect overpriced motels next 42 miles," or "Most expensive gasoline in Maine next exit."

If you owned a tacky gift shop, an overpriced motel, or a price-gouging service station—wouldn't you be concerned?

The other story I read in the newspaper was about the state's plan to open a slick new discount liquor store in Kittery.

What ever happened to the oft-expressed good intention of getting the state out of the liquor business? For more years than I care to remember, politicians of both parties support- ed the idea of getting the state out of the liquor business. Governor Angus King, for one, has consistently opposed state-run liquor stores. But despite all those good intentions, the state is nowhere near selling off its booze operation. Not only that, but according to this newspaper article, state offi- cials now want the state liquor store in Kittery to be easier to find so people driving through can get off the highway and stock up with lots of discount moonshine.

Dennis Bailey, Governor King's spokesman, claims that it is an awkward position philosophically. The governor dis- agrees with the state retailing liquor, but on the other hand, he's a businessman. So if you're going to stay in business, you have to maximize profits.

Say what?

Here is something—selling booze—that the governor says the state shouldn't be doing at all. But he says something like: We shouldn't be selling this stuff, but by gory, as long as we cannot stop it, I'm going to see to it that we sell as much of it as we can.

But we all know the real problem is our boozy neigh- bor to the south—New Hampshire. Those folks have no intention—good or otherwise—of getting out of the liquor business. And those grog merchants in New Hampshire sure know how to push the spirits. They shame the poor State of Maine at every turn, and our state officials don't like it one bit.

The feeling is, if New Hampshire has a giant discount liquor store right there on their freeway with a well-marked, easy-on, easy-off ramp (so that not even drunks will miss it), then Maine should have one too. For all I know they might even be planning to have a drive-through cocktail lounge.

But, who knows? Maybe they're planning to pave our roads with all the profits.

Someone once said something like: "Show me a man of 25 who is not a liberal, and I will show you a man who has no heart. Show me a man of 50 who is not a conservative, and I will show you a man who has no brain."

The quote has been variously attributed to a host of political types, including Winston Churchill. It's not really important to me to know who said it, and I'm not even saying here that I agree wholeheartedly with the quote. But I don't think it's revealing a shocking secret to say that people tend to become a tad more conservative as they get older.

I thought of the above quote (and a few others that I dare not include in this wholesome family book) when a press release from the Maine Department of Labor came across the transom here at Storyteller Central.

According to the release, the state will receive more than $3.5 million from the federal government to help retrain Maine fishermen and their families. Governor Angus King explained in the press release that the federal grant "will help us double our efforts to help those who will be transitioning from the sea to land-based jobs."

First of all, Maine must be changing faster than I knew because I can't imagine any Maine fisherman I've ever known admitting to anyone in public that he was preparing to go and do something called "transitioning." Then I wondered how the average Maine fisherman would use a word like "transitioning" in a sentence? And how would such a sentence sound down there on the commercial fishing docks at five in the morning?

"Well, Earl, this could be my last fishing trip aboard the *Ester T*. Beginning Monday, I've decided to take advantage of that big government program the governor's been talking about, and I'm gonna start 'transitioning' from a sea to a land-based job."

In the past, even if you managed to find a Maine fisherman who admitted to engaging in a transitioning activity, he certainly wouldn't have been too public about it nor expected the federal government to pay for it. In the past, when someone in a Maine maritime family was, as the governor would say, transitioning from the sea to a land-based job, it usually meant that he and Mother were either planning to open a Mom & Pop store in town or they were packing up and moving to Connecticut.

Over the years, lots of men here in Maine have retired from the sea and gotten jobs on land. The government almost never had anything to say or do about it.

According to Labor Commissioner Valerie R. Landry, whose department applied for the grant, the federal money will be used for all kinds of things besides retraining these old salts for jobs on land. There's also lots of money to provide things like "outreach" and "recruitment."

Now, I know enough about the language of the bureaucrat to know that outreach means something like going out and beating the bushes in order to find these fishermen. I would imagine that recruitment means sitting down and talking to them, getting them to agree to this transitioning business, and then signing them up for government goodies. There's also some federal money for something called "assessment," and a little money left over for "planning," and finally a dollar or two for "readjustment" and "retraining."

On the Great Seal of the State of Maine there are two fellas standing there with the tools of their trade. In the modern language of government one could be said to be employed in a land-based job (farming) and the other in a sea-based job (merchant seaman or fisherman).

How many fishermen have to go through this transitioning business before that famous fella on our state's seal is also a candidate for transitioning?

I can just see it now. The legislature will come up with a new character for our state seal. He'll be dressed smartly as a fully transitioned, land-based agent for all your real estate and insurance needs. And all done with your tax dollars.

I must be getting old.

As I write this week's column, the Big Election has not occurred. And rather than make daring predictions about how I think the various races will turn out, I thought I'd just reminisce about elections gone by.

A Moose and a Lobster Walk into a Bar . . .

Every time election season rolls around I think of home, and I begin to recall with fondness those hotly contested elections we had there years ago. It's a wonder anyone in that town is still speaking.

Every Election Day in our small town, no matter what else we'd vote on, we always had a vote on alcohol. Some years it was a vote on Sunday sales, and other years it was a vote on wine and spirits or public drunkenness. It was always something.

The various alcohol questions divided the town like no other issue. Our town meetings were like prayer meetings when compared to the bitter civic battles fought over the sale and use of alcohol.

The anti-alcohol forces were led by the Tuttle family and their patriarch Hollis Tuttle, a pillar of the local church. Throughout his life, Hollis Tuttle did everything he could to keep demon rum out of our town and out of the bloodstream of everyone in it. The pro-alcohol forces spent years just getting beer into our local store. But wine continued to be voted down. When I moved away in 1981, you still couldn't buy wine in our town, and you couldn't buy any beer on Sundays, which created a weekly traffic jam in the parking lot of the beer store located just over our town line.

A story about the last days of Hollis Tuttle almost caused a scandal in the anti-alcohol forces.

Hollis Tuttle's doctor, a Bangor specialist, told the Tuttle family that their father was not well, and probably didn't have long to live. The good doctor said the only thing that might help him live longer would be a double shot of whiskey twice a day.

"Now, I know your family's views on alcohol," said the doctor, "and I only tell you about the whiskey because I am ethically bound to inform you of all the medicinal options at your disposal. If you decide to give your father the whiskey, you could put it in a glass of milk, and he'd never know the difference."

The doctor even suggested that they buy a cow to keep in the barn behind the house. And then they could tell the father that the cow's fresh milk was particularly healthy for him at this time in his life.

Once the doctor informed the family of their options, he said it was their decision and he would not bring up the subject again.

After long, painful discussions, the Tuttles finally decided to do as the doctor recommended, and put the medicinal whiskey into their father's milk two times a day. They also went out and bought a cow. They told him the cow was very special and produced especially healthy milk. The whiskey-and-milk treatment kept the senior Tuttle quite healthy for some time, and the family never breathed a word about what he was really drinking.

But one day he began to deteriorate, and eventually, he was near death. As his final hour approached, the whole family gathered at his bedside. Getting weaker by the minute, the old man finally motioned to his eldest son, who came to hear his father's dying words.

As the son leaned over, the patriarch looked him in the eye and said, "Son, whatever you do, don't ever sell that wonderful cow."

Just when you thought you'd heard your last outhouse joke, the folks at the National Park Service come up with a real knee-slapper.

According to an Associated Press article from Delaware Water Gap, Pennsylvania—unknown in outhouse circles as a source of humor until recently—hikers now have the use of a two-hole outhouse that cost the federal government (meaning us taxpayers) more than $333,000. Kinda gives a whole new meaning to the phrase "bureaucratic waste."

These lavish trailside bathrooms feature a gabled slate roof, cedar clapboard siding, cottage-style porches and a cobblestone foundation that can withstand an earthquake—which is one of the first features I look for in my preferred outhouses.

Apparently, included in the cost of this fancy federal outhouse was about $102,000 for planning and design and $81,000 for an on-site engineer.

Can't you see the entry on this engineer fella's updated resume?

"1996-97—On-site engineer for deluxe two-hole federal outhouse in Pennsylvania."

Now, remember, this is an outhouse we're talking about. Maine used to be thick with all kinds of outhouses, humble structures that once stood behind most every house in rural Maine. Now, sure this federal outhouse is a two-holer, and granted, your two-holers are always going to be a bit more uptown and costly than your lowly single-holer—but I think most of us here in Maine would agree that no matter how many holes we're talking about, $333,000 is a tad more than your average outhouse ought to cost. I'd be willing to bet that if you added up the cost of every outhouse built in the state of Maine in the last 150 years you wouldn't come anywhere near this $333,000 figure.

Back home, when I was a kid, many wobbly outhouses on stilts lined our riverbank (never mind what river). Anyway, every year around Halloween some kids would get into mischief and go around tipping over outhouses. Among my friends, Thurland Beal was probably the best outhouse tipper around. As I heard it, after one busy night of outhouse tipping, Thurland's father called him downstairs for questioning. His father wanted to know if Thurland knew anything about who tipped over the family's outhouse the previous night. Remembering a lesson from history that he had just learned in school, Thurland bravely answered his father by saying:

"Father, I cannot tell a lie. I tipped over the family outhouse last night."

With that, his father took him to the woodshed for some old-fashioned discipline. When his father had finished, Thurland said: "What did you do that for, Dad? When our first president George Washington was a young boy, he chopped down his father's cherry tree, and when George told his father the truth, his father praised him for his truthfulness and didn't punish him. How come you punished me for telling you the truth about the family outhouse?"

"Well, son," the father answered, "I'd be willing to bet that George Washington's father wasn't sitting there in that cherry tree when George chopped it down."

A Moose and a Lobster Walk into a Bar . . .

A rich fella back home, Asa Tingley, once hired an $80-an-hour consultant from the big city of Portland to help him make his business more profitable. The expert arrived from the prosperous south in a fancy new car, wearing a fancy-looking suit, and carrying a fine-looking leather briefcase. The prosperous-looking expert started right off asking Asa some clever, consultant-type questions.

"So, Mr. Tingley, how many people would you say you have working here at your company at any given time?"

"Oh, about half of them," said Asa.

"I see," said the expert, scribbling the answer down on his impressive-looking yellow legal pad. "And how many of your employees would you say are approaching retirement?"

"I'd say all of them are heading in that direction," Asa replied.

I thought of Asa and just had to chuckle a bit the other day when I picked up the newspaper and read that not one, but two, of these high-paid consultants had been hired by a well-meaning group in a town up north. Somebody had the idea that these consultants might be able to halt the quarreling among those hearty north country folks over how the local school educates the town's children. This newspaper article claims the folks in this small town have been quarreling "for months" about teaching methods used in the community school. It was pretty clear to me that this newspaper fella didn't know a whole lot about small Maine towns.

Did you catch that business about quarreling for months? I don't know about you, but in the town I come from, folks have been arguing about the school and every other thing for as long as anyone can remember. When folks in our town stop arguing about things like schools, they'll turn right around and argue about the town's roads, the town dump, the Board of Selectmen, the library, the town budget, the shape the town's buildings are in, the artwork on the cover of the town report—and just about anything else that can be argued about. But no matter what else the townspeople are fighting over, there's always a special fondness for arguments about the town's school.

When the topic of schools comes up in town, the arguments are unending. Folks first argue about whether to build a new school. When that is sort of decided, they start arguing about how big the school should be. When those questions are mostly decided they argue about where to put it and whether it should be built of brick or wood and where to buy the materials. Once the arguments about the outside are settled they start arguing about the inside and whether the new school should have black or green chalkboards in the classrooms. The arguments never stop.

We had a school board meeting years ago that almost came to blows over whether the school should have those desks that are bolted to the floor or those kind that just slide around the room. And if I went into the store back home even now, I bet I could still get into a good argument with somebody about what they're teaching the kids in the school these days or about the teachers they're hiring, or the new principal.

According to this newspaper article, the two consultants—one from Portland and another from Boston—want to help residents get over the acrimony and rebuild a sense of community. Sounds like they're trying to destroy the place.

These consultants claimed they would act as "facilitators."

I asked a friend of mine who knows most everything what a facilitator was, and he said it was someone you hired when you thought you should be having a meeting about something but had no idea why. So you hire a facilitator who is specially trained to think up all kinds of reasons why you should have a meeting—instead of doing something useful. If you pay them enough, they'll do up the whole meeting in good shape and send you an impressive report on it. You won't even have to go—but it will cost you a lot of money.

Anyway, one of these consultants upcountry said that whatever happens in the town will take some time. Should anyone be surprised? If I were making what these experts are making, I'd probably want it to take some time, too. I don't doubt that these facilitators will eventually get these small-town folks to stop arguing about schools for a while because they'll be having too much fun arguing about whose idea it was to hire these fancy-talking $80-an-hour facilitators from the city in the first place.

I read in the paper the other day an article about the Down East town of Cherryfield. Around wild blueberry circles, Cherryfield is known as the Wild Blueberry Capital of the World. Don't misunderstand me here: It's not the circles that are wild, or the blueberry growers that are wild—it's the blueberries, we're told, that are wild. The growers themselves are a pretty sober and serious bunch. Anyway, Cherryfield wants to solidify its position in these same blueberry circles and attract hordes of wealthy tourists by building what most likely will be the world's first wild blueberry museum, right there in the middle of town. Cherryfield wants to be for wild blueberry lovers what New York City is for pastrami-on-rye lovers; what New Orleans is for shrimp fans; or what Boston is to baked bean buffs.

Business leaders there in Cherryfield believe the lowly, unassuming wild blueberry can do for Cherryfield what the earmuff has done for Farmington; what the wooden clothespin has done for West Paris; what the toothpick has done for Wilton.

The hope in Cherryfield and the surrounding area is that if you build the world's first museum dedicated exclusively to the lowly wild blueberry, the tourists will come flocking to it. People the world over who have always loved the wild blueberry and have sought in various awkward ways to learn more about it will now be able to beat a path to Cherryfield's door, so to speak. Before long, numerous inns, hotels, B & Bs, restaurants and all kinds of other tourist businesses will naturally spring up to house and feed these hungry hordes from around the world.

Having been around a little myself I know that in today's complex society, ideas like wild blueberry museums don't just pop up out of nowhere. I now know they're likely to pop up in sparsely populated places like Cherryfield. But according to the newspaper article I read, there's more to the story. It turns out that the whole idea of building a wild blueberry museum come from the offices of the Down East Resource Conservation and Development Council. The council spends its time thinking of ways to bring tourists and economic development to the Down East area. After hiring consultants and facilitators it was determined that the area wasn't doing enough with the wild blueberries. Sure, they grew them and harvested them and froze them and sold them to customers around the world. But they could do so much more. After many more meetings and brainstorming sessions, they finally decided what else they could do and the idea for a wild blueberry museum was born. Recently, the council was awarded a $3,000 grant for the museum project from the Maine Community Foundation, and will use the money to pay an architect to design them a museum.

I don't know what you think about this, but I was really surprised. Shocked, even. Not surprised or shocked that folks would want to build a museum to honor the wild blueberry, but surprised to learn that you could get an architect to design you a museum for as little as $3,000. If that's the case, and we'll just have to assume for the moment that it is, then small towns all over Maine can have artistically designed museums built to honor one crop or invention or oddity or another that has made that town kinda famous. Farmington can draw hordes of tourists with its earmuff museum—if it doesn't have one already. West Paris can build a museum to tell the people of the world the wonderful story of the wooden clothespin; Freeport can design a museum to honor the outlet store; Port Clyde's museum could honor the tasty sardine; Wells can build a museum to honor the tollbooth; Kittery, the discount liquor store.

The possibilities are only limited by a town's collective imagination and, of course, a budget of $3,000 for a good architectural design.

Whenever it gets to be election time, I always think of home.

Our Down East town was known, among other things, as the most Republican town in Maine, which was not an easy title to claim when you consider how Republican our small towns used to be.

We'd have an election back home, and when they'd count them up, there'd be 393 Republican ballots and no Democrat ballots. No Democratic ballot had ever been cast in our little town, or if it had, the officials had never bothered to count it, believing it just some sick joke.

Then, sometime in the early 1960s, around the time of the famous Kennedy versus Nixon election, someone from way down south retired from the navy and bought a house right in the center of town. Being as how he was used to the hustle and bustle of the city, he wanted to be on Main Street, right there in the middle of things.

He was the nicest fella you'd ever want to meet. Couldn't do enough for his neighbors or the town.

But some folks soon noticed him acting a bit peculiar, and some began to suspect that he had a dark side.

The first Election Day after his arrival came and everyone went to vote. No one noticed anything too strange. This navy fella showed up at the polls and voted like everyone else. He even chatted with the poll workers and then went home.

It wasn't until that night, after the polls had closed and the town officials went down to Town Hall to count up the ballots, that they realized what exactly had happened in their beloved town that day: The votes totaled 393 Republican—and 1 Democrat.

The officials were stunned. Their mouths went dry. You could have knocked any one of them over with a seagull feather. They sat across from each other, staring in total disbelief.

Just like that, the town's title—"The Most Republican Town in Maine"—was shattered. Gone, like a Democrat's campaign promise.

Some officials had harbored deep fears that such a thing could happen, what with all the people from away moving into small towns. Now, here it was, bold as brass; right in front of their quivering noses, someone had actually voted Democrat.

You didn't have to hit any of the town officials upside the head with a two-by-four. They knew that this navy fella from the deep south, probably Massachusetts, must have been the wicked voter.

It wasn't long before the newcomer figured he'd done something very wrong, but he couldn't quite figure out what. While everyone in town was still friendly to him—because he was still the nicest person you'd want to meet—he sensed something was off with how they regarded him. How could he have known that with the flick of a lever in a voting booth, he had robbed the town of its precious title and unexpectedly revealed his dark secret and unfortunate character flaw?

He began to feel anxious and his blood pressure soared. He went to the doctor, but it didn't help. After several months of this, folks say he finally did the only decent and gracious thing he could have done under the circumstances—he died.

No one dared mention it, but everyone knew that with his passing the town would once again reclaim its title of "The Most Republican Town in Maine."

To show how much they appreciated his fine gesture on their behalf, the townspeople gave him the finest funeral in the town's history.

By coincidence, the day after the funeral was another Election Day. Everyone went off to vote, and town officials went to the Town Hall after the election to count up the ballots: 392 Republican and 1 Democrat.

The officials were dumbfounded and turned white as ghosts.

Elmer Beal, the second selectman, who was also the town's undertaker, rose to his feet, stumbled toward the door and mumbled to himself: "Good heavens, we buried the wrong man!"

CHAPTER FIVE

I'm Glad You Asked

O ne thing about being a newspaper columnist and frequent storyteller around Maine is that I get asked lots of questions. Fortunately, I have a lot of answers—not always the best answers, but answers nonetheless. Over the years, I have used these answers in an attempt to enlighten folks about our great state.

F or example, Steve, from "somewhere out west," was vacationing in Maine with his family and wrote:

"This is our first time in Maine, and we've been fascinated by just about everything we've seen so far—Baxter State Park, Acadia, Old Orchard Beach—but we are also a little confused by some of the things we've come across while visiting your state.

"Last weekend, for example, we were driving through several mid-Maine towns, and in one stretch of about twelve miles, we must have passed no fewer than nine yard sales, six flea markets, several garage and barn sales and at least one tag sale. Well, we

didn't exactly 'pass' all these sales; we had to stop and browse at every single one of them looking for bargains.

"I became confused, John, because after about the sixth sale I couldn't tell why these folksy, informal enterprises had different names. Each sale was pretty much the same as all the rest, and each sale operator was selling the same kinds of items—furniture, lamps, rugs, kitchen items, books and clothes.

"To confuse things a little more, all the yard sales were also selling items out of their garages or barns, the garage sales all had items being sold in their yards, and the items at all the sales had tags on them.

"Are there subtle differences in all these sales that I'm not aware of?"

Thanks for the letter, Steve. The word *subtle* is probably not the best word to describe the almost imperceptible differences between flea markets and yard sales and the like. Maine's folksy-looking backyard retail businesses are the result of highly sophisticated marketing studies and techniques that have been developed and implemented here in Maine over the last century. In that time, these shrewd down-home retailers have spent years studying and researching market trends, demographics, incomes and consumer attitudes and have greatly improved the variety of their quaint products and the efficiency of their sales operations.

The average visitor to these sales merely sees furniture, books, or kitchen items; but over the years these sly salesmen have developed exciting new products, opened a variety of new markets, and made their hand-lettered advertising posters much more effective.

To the untrained eye, those folks who hold yard sales or tag sales are just the people next door trying to make a little less clutter and a little more room in a house or trailer. But if you promise not to tell anyone, Steve, I'll let you know that nothing could be further from the truth: These people are having a sale for the same reason Ames or Wal-Mart have sales—to unload tons of merchandise on unsuspecting customers like you, Steve!

These skilled rural merchandisers have been at this highly competitive business for a long time, and what may seem to be a random name to someone like you, Steve, is actually a name chosen with great care after much careful research.

Maybe the next time you slow down in front of a "yard full of junk," Steve, you'll show a little more respect, huh?

Peter, from "somewhere along the coast," e-mailed the following:

"John, I'm what you might call a traveling salesman, or commercial traveler, as we prefer to be called. The past few seasons here in Vacationland have been pretty rough on folks like me who have to travel to make a living. Do you know it now costs well over $100 for any kind of motel room along the coast from July to Labor Day? The other day I registered at a motel in one of Maine's more popular coastal towns, and the clerk said, 'That'll be $143.70, with tax. That price, of course, includes our "free" continental breakfast.' Where do they get off charging me all that money and then—with a straight face—telling me my breakfast is FREE?

"And while we're on the subject of tourist season, John, how come I keep seeing fancy color ads in national magazines that feature our state and its many tourist attractions? There's not

enough room now for the cars we have on Route 1 in the sum-
mer. Where are we supposed to put the gaggle of tourists that
these expensive ads are sure to bring?"

I hear you, Peter.

Believe me, I, too, have driven those same crowded coastal roads and stood in those same motel offices and listened
to those same clerks tell me that my $150 room comes with
a "free" Danish and coffee.

But, Peter, I have also listened to my friends in the tourist
business who remind me—as I'm thinking about my free
$150 Danish and cup of coffee—how important tourism is
to our state's economy. They say, "Sure, John, the coast is
crowded, but northern and western Maine hardly ever see
a real, living, breathing, credit-card-wielding tourist. If it
weren't for those fancy magazine ads, John, they wouldn't
even know what a tourist looked like."

I don't know how long you've been in Maine, Peter, but
debates about tourists and their effect on life as we know it
here in Maine go back a long way.

My Uncle Abner was born Down East in 1878, and he
used to tell about the flocks of tourists that poured into the
state back in the 1890s.

Back in the late 1950s when my Uncle Abner would hear
about some ordinary motel along the coast that was charging
$8 a night for a room he'd just scoff.

Uncle Abner would listen to people complaining, and
then launch into a story about the old days. He said back
then people wouldn't come racing up an overcrowded turnpike to Maine, or go crawling along in slow-moving traffic
through one coastal town after another.

Uncle Abner liked to tell about people arriving in Maine
in comfort aboard something like the beautiful 241-foot

paddlewheel steamer *State of Maine*, a well-known passenger steamer built in Bath in 1881.

When he was a kid, you could get a fine room in a grand coastal resort for a few dollars a night, but most everyone stayed for weeks at time. All meals were included.

For breakfast, according to Uncle Abner, you would be offered sausage, bacon, steak, eggs, toast, cornbread, muffins, pastries, pancakes, pork chops and fried potatoes. There'd also be gallons of mineral water, orange juice and coffee to wash it all down.

If you lingered too long at the breakfast table you could then enjoy snacks that were served around 11:30 a.m.

Lunch—consisting of all kinds of cold cuts, breads, rolls, fried chicken, fish, all kinds of salads and desserts—was served around 12:30.

For those who still had room left, there was always afternoon tea served around three.

After tea, you'd have several hours of "free time" before dinner was served. Most people spent the time playing tennis or croquet, or were out on the bay sailing. The less active guests would just sit on the porch and talk or read.

As incredible as it may sound, Uncle Abner said the food served all day from breakfast through teatime was nothing when compared to what was to come. Dinnertime was when your typical fancy resort really dragged out piles of food, and the typical guest really got down to some serious eating.

He said you might start off your evening meal with oysters, or clam chowder, or crabs, maybe a bowl of turtle soup, followed by a nice baked fish, a few lobsters, roast duck, a thick steak and all kinds of fresh-picked vegetables.

When all that was cleared away, there would be coffee and desserts and cigars for the men and chocolates for the ladies.

A Moose and a Lobster Walk into a Bar . . .

Kinda makes today's free coffee and doughnut sound a little pathetic, doesn't it?

Of course, back in those days, with lots of free bacon and such, the life expectancy was about 57.

Vanessa in Scarborough writes: *"John, while waiting for the first passenger train to arrive here in Maine, I was sitting in my car near the tracks listening to the radio, and heard someone going on and on with pretty negative comments about the train. In all their jabbering they really didn't say anything of substance or interest, as far as I was concerned. What caught my ear in the long-winded discourse was the radio guy's use of the word 'boondoggle,' which he spouted several times in his diatribe. I know you don't get political in your column, John, so I won't ask what you think of the return of passenger train service. But, I do know that you often get into the meaning of obscure words. Tell me, John, what do you know about the word 'boondoggle'?"*

Thanks for the e-mail, Vanessa. Speaking of words, the one most often used to describe a person who talks a lot but says very little is windbag, so I hope it wasn't me you were listening to.

Even though I'm not a politician—I've never run for anything (not even a train) and have no plans to run for political office—I do know something about the origin of boondoggle.

On April 3, 1935, Robert C. Marshall, a witness before a congressional committee investigating the Relief Administration in New York City, testified that he was hired by the head of some government program to teach various crafts, including boondoggling, to workers on relief.

Anticipating questions from the congressmen, Mr. Marshall then went on to describe boondoggling as the art or craft of making useful items known as boondoggles.

As expected, inquiring minds on the committee then wanted to know what a boondoggle was.

According to Marshall, a boondoggle was any useful gadget or article that resulted from practicing the ancient craft of boondoggling.

That, Vanessa, is the historical part of this story and can be referenced in *The Dictionary of American History.*

The following is what I imagine happened after Mr. Marshall's informative testimony:

Sleepy reporters at the hearing began to stir and talk among themselves.

"What was that word the witness just mumbled?" they asked.

"I think he said 'boondoggle,' or something like that," was the reply they got.

The word boondoggle became an instant hit across the country in both craft and political circles. Why not? It was such a great word! People loved saying it.

The artsy-crafty crowd was at first stunned to learn of this new "craft." "Why didn't anyone tell us?" they all wanted to know.

Then they demanded to know more about it. Posh boondoggling schools opened across the land. Art schools, trying to catch up, began offering boondoggling majors.

Clever politicians, always on the lookout for new phrases, immediately began using the newly coined word to ridicule any government program they thought of as useless or unproductive—which, of course, turned out to be any gov-

ernment program that didn't spend bushel baskets full of tax money in their congressional district.

Several readers have written to ask about earmuff inventor Chester Greenwood with questions like, *"When is Chester Greenwood Day?" "Did he really invent the earmuff?" "Is he famous for anything else?"*

Well, as far as we know, Chester Greenwood Day is still celebrated each year on the first Saturday in December in the Franklin County shire town of Farmington.

Besides the earmuff, Mr. Greenwood is credited with giving our bumpy world the shock absorber. Not knowing much more than that about the inventive guy, I figure he must have been involved somehow in the summer tourist trade and needed another business to make money and occupy his time during our long winters. He obviously wanted his off-season business to be one that would do well in the cold weather. After contemplating our long, cold winters with their bitter cold winds and frost-heaved roads, he must have concluded that earmuffs and shock absorbers were the way to go.

As far as being famous for other things—if you're known throughout Maine as the inventor of the earmuff and the shock absorber, do you really need any more feathers in your cap?

From Susan in Portland comes the following: *"Hi, John. I was told you were great at rooting out the derivation of words or phrases. I'm looking for the original meaning of 'chip on your shoulder.'"*

Thank you for the email, Susan. It's nice to read that I'm considered great at something.

I don't need a dictionary of phrases to rattle off the meaning of "chip off the old block," or even the more obscure phrase, "giving someone the cold shoulder," but the phrase "chip on your shoulder" required a little poking around.

In case you're wondering, the first phrase means the "chip," or son, looks just like the "block," or dad, that produced him. To give the phrase more weight than it probably deserves, some people have been known to call their sons Chip.

As for the second expression, giving someone the cold shoulder—in England years ago, when a guest overstayed his welcome, some hosts would drop a not-too-subtle hint by giving the bloke a cold shoulder of meat for dinner instead of a beautifully roasted prime cut like the one they served him upon his arrival.

According to some references the expression "chip on your shoulder" is American in origin and refers to a nineteenth century form of challenge where you dared someone to knock a wood chip off your shoulder. If the person knocked the chip off, you would either do nothing about it or haul off and slug the individual, which would then cause a fight, I guess.

A Moose and a Lobster Walk into a Bar . . .

Mike from Bath writes: *"John, do you remember the public television show,* So You Think You Know Maine? *What ever happened to that show? Did they ever put out a board game? My great-grandmother loved all kinds of games and collected quite a few. I'm trying to remember if she ever had a Maine game in her vast collection. She was from Searsport, but spent much of her childhood aboard her father's hen frigate, Alice Way. She'd often talk about the board games they had back then and how different they were from the modern games we played as kids. Now, it's my turn to tell the younger relatives about games like the one public television used to broadcast. Anything you can tell me will be appreciated."*

Thanks for the letter, Mike. The first thing to jump out at me from your letter was the term *hen frigate*, which I hadn't heard in a while. In fact we seldom hear about hen frigates in these enlightened times, Mike.

Hen frigates, according to John Gould's *Maine Lingo*, were sailing vessels on which the skipper's wife and family accompanied him at sea. In the late 1800s and early 1900s, Maine-based hen frigates sailed the world, and would often be spotted in foreign ports rafted together so that the families could socialize.

As for the rest of your letter, Mike, there may have been a board game based on the popular game show about Maine, but I don't remember seeing one.

In 1984, Neil Rolde wrote a book based on the show, and you might still be able to find a copy in your local library.

I remember the host of the show would ask a panel of four eager contestants questions like: "Eben Jordan was born on a farm in Danville, Maine, in the year 1822. At the age of fourteen, he left Maine with $3 in his pocket and later founded what famous Boston firm?"

The answer, of course, is the Jordan Marsh Company. I know because I was a contestant on the show a few times and that was one of the questions I got right.

Another question I managed to answer was: "What is the only hyphenated town in Maine?" The answer is: Dover-Foxcroft.

Jean from West Falmouth writes: *"John, a friend from Georgia was visiting this fall, and we spent some time shopping. At an antique mall up your way in Oxford, I saw a sideboard and mentioned it to my friend.*

"'Did you notice that nice sideboard in one of the middle aisles?' I asked.

"'Sideboard? Whatever are you talking about? What's a sideboard?' he replied.

"When I took him to see it, he said, 'Sideboard? That's a buffet.'

"He said he'd heard of sidearms, sideburns, sidelines and sidekicks. And from Martha Stewart he's learned more than he really wanted to know about side dishes. But in all his years he'd never heard of a sideboard, and wondered where the word came from. John, help us out, here. Where does the word sideboard come from? Is it just a New England word for buffet?"

Thanks for the nice letter, Jean.

I don't know if it's just a regional word, but a sideboard, as most of us know, is a piece of dining room furniture used

for storing dishes and linen, and is sometimes called a buf-fet—or as the French would say—*boo-fay*.

I don't happen to be one of them but many people think of English as a common-sounding language and if you want something to sound really classy you have to add a little French to it. That's why, when you're having a fancy dinner you don't serve snacks before the meal, instead you serve your guests *hors d'oeuvres*.

The same applies to furniture. In English we have words like "old-fashioned" or "used" to describe furniture that's been around a few years. But who's going to pay you top dollar for used furniture?

Employ a fancy French word like "antique" to describe the old stuff, and then double the effect by calling the item an "antique boo-fay," and suddenly it's worth all kinds of money.

That's the best I can come up with, Jean.

Al Crimmons from Canton, Ohio writes: *"John, I visit-ed your lovely state for the first time recently while on a business trip to the northeast, and as I traveled up the coast of Maine from Portland to Belfast, visiting customers along the way, I managed to come across your delightful column in several different newspapers. Fortunately for me, three of the newspapers were running different columns of yours in the editions I saw, so I was able to get a good taste for your point of view and your writing, and I must say, I enjoyed it all very much.*

"*Without getting too corny or philosophical here, I have to say that after reading your columns, I came away with the idea that you are very proud of your region and your state, and the 'rugged individuals' who inhabit it. From your columns I also got the distinct idea that you are probably the best person to explain to me—a proud Midwesterner—what the term 'Yankee Ingenuity' means. It is an expression that the rest of the country most often associates with the people of New England and one that I have wondered about for some time. I just wanted a 'professional' explanation of what it might mean.*"

Thank you, Al, for your kind letter. It's always good to read nice things from readers who enjoy my column—even if it's a reader who is just passing through the state.

Let me also say that although I've been through parts of Ohio over the years in my travels, I must admit that the only thing I know about Canton, Ohio is that it is mentioned by the Stage Manager in Thornton Wilder's *Our Town* where at an early point in the play, he tells the audience: "Doc Gibbs died in 1930. The new hospital's named after him. Mrs. Gibbs died first—long time ago, in fact. She went out to visit her daughter in Canton, Ohio, and died there—pneumonia—but her body was brought back here."

I happen to know these lines well, Al, because beginning in high school in the 1960s, and a few times since then, I have played the role of the Stage Manager in several productions of *Our Town*—the most recent being the 1997 production at Bates College.

But enough rambling on about places in Ohio and productions at Bates.

As I thought about your specific question, Al, I looked out the window in my neat but not overly ostentatious office here at Storyteller Central. Gazing across the snow-covered and frozen river, I thought almost immediately of an "ingenious Yankee" named Captain William Bradstreet.

Captain Who? I hear a chorus of readers ask.

Well, in the winter of 1824 Captain William Bradstreet found himself icebound on the Kennebec somewhere near Pittston. His brig *Orion* had not made him a penny all winter, and he was more than a little annoyed by the whole situation.

As spring thaw began (which it should be doing here any month now) and the ice began to break up, Captain Bradstreet was ready to head south. Adding to the long list of things that were aggravating him was the fact that his first loading port was Baltimore, so he would be sailing over 600 miles with no cargo.

Today some chirpy individual might quote to Captain Bradstreet that overused expression: "When life gives you lemons, make lemonade." And Captain Bradstreet probably would have promptly thrown that irritating person overboard.

But at some point in his journey down the Kennebec, Captain Bradstreet came up with the "ingenious" idea of making lemonade (just kidding). His idea was to fill his hold with some of the huge chunks of ice that surrounded his vessel and blocked his passage.

Once filled—with a cargo that had cost him nothing— Captain Bradstreet sailed his brig on to Baltimore. We're told that this first commercial shipment of ice was sold in Baltimore by the captain for $700. And those, of course, were 1820s dollars, which we must always assume were a whole lot different in looks and value from our present-day greenbacks.

You can just imagine, Al, what ship owners along the Kennebec began thinking once they heard what crafty Captain Bradstreet was able to get for his load of free ice.

Ice—the stuff that had been clogging up shipping lanes and causing all kinds of mischief on the river for years—was apparently valuable. All you had to do was cut it, load it and haul it to someplace like Baltimore—where summers were long and hot, and food spoiled easily.

They say the next winter, the brig *Criterion* sailed out of Bath bound for Havana, Cuba with 160 tons of crystal-clear Kennebec ice in her hold.

Maine's commercial ice business had begun.

As the industry grew, shipowners began using another seemingly useless commodity—sawdust—to pack around their ice as insulation. Pretty ingenious, huh?

I don't know if I've answered your question, Al, about the phrase "Yankee ingenuity," but I hope you've enjoyed my answer as much as I enjoyed telling it.

A l from Popham writes: *"Okay, John, so I'm not from Maine; I'm a flatlandah, and don't know a whole lot about your history, but it sounds to me like you Mainers can't get along with your neighbors. Over the past year or so I've been reading about how Maine is arguing with New Hampshire over the exact location of the state line. And didn't you go to war with England a while back (the Aroostook War) over the precise location of your northern boundary? I didn't know Maine people were so pushy.*

"I bring this up because I'm now in the middle of a property line dispute with my neighbor here in Popham. It appears to me

that Mainers like to fight about such things. Why can't we all just get along, John?"

Thanks for the letter, Al. A good question.

After reading your letter, I began thinking about my own land deals over the years and realized that of the six pieces of property my wife and I have owned since we were married, we've been involved in minor boundary disputes with three of them.

Now, anyone who knows me can tell you that I'm about as easy a guy to get along with as you're likely to find in or out of Maine, so we know it's nothing I did that caused the land disputes, right?

Right?

If you had read the papers more carefully, Al, you would have read somewhere that the border dispute with New Hampshire was settled recently when the U.S. Supreme Court said, in effect, "The present border looks hunky-dory to us just the way it is," and threw the dispute out of court. Or more simply, "Maine wins!"

But don't worry, Al. Knowing our neighbors to the west it won't be long before they'll be at it again with another border dispute.

The Aroostook War was an undeclared and bloodless war that almost flared up because England and the United States couldn't agree on where the border was between our country and the province of New Brunswick. Since way back, the Brits had claimed all the land above Mars Hill.

I can hear cynical readers now saying, "And we were prepared to fight for whatever's above Mars Hill?"

In a word—yes.

We had just about had it with the British by this time, so in January of 1839, a land agent named Rufus McIntire took a posse into the disputed area and started arresting Canadian lumberjacks who were cutting trees on the disputed land.

As you might expect, Rufus was arrested by the Canadians, and then Mainers started getting a tad annoyed.

Within two months there were 10,000 Maine troops either encamped along the Aroostook River or marching toward the spot.

In Washington, the federal government authorized a force of 50,000 men and $10 million in the event of war. That's how much we cared about the land above Mars Hill.

The British, convinced that they'd stirred up a hornet's nest, decided to talk peace and eventually signed the Webster-Ashburton Treaty in 1842, which set the line between us.

Let's look at some local "legends." Among the letters and emails that arrive each week here at Storyteller Central, there are always a few from curious readers who seek to know with total certainty whether a certain story they heard or read is "really true."

Regular readers will recall the story we told about someone from Arizona who received an express shipment of beautiful Maine lobsters as a gift, and proceeded to throw them in the garbage because they were all dark-colored and not bright red the way fresh lobsters are supposed to be.

We questioned the truth of the story, and asked readers to let us know if they ever heard of someone—even in Arizona—being so ignorant of things like the color of live Maine lobsters.

A Moose and a Lobster Walk into a Bar . . .

Within a week there was a flood of mail from all over the state, detailing similar lobster stories involving people in the South, Midwest—all over.

A lobster dealer on the coast took the time to write a long letter explaining that he deals with the problem of the color of live lobsters all the time. And yes, the stories you hear about people throwing live lobsters out because they weren't bright red, are true.

Okay, so that one turned out to be true. But the email we got this week from an inquisitive reader makes us a tad doubtful. Let me know what you think.

Carol from Northport writes: *"John, I heard this story and first thought it was just too preposterous to be true. Then I figured you'd know if there were any truth to it. A friend who works in Bar Harbor during the summer assures me it really happened.*

"According to my friend, a shoplifter in the fish department of the Shop 'n Save in Bar Harbor took two live lobsters out of the tank, stuffed them in his baggy pants, and headed for the door. Before reaching the checkout counters, the man dropped to the floor and began writhing in pain. It was later learned that one of the lobsters had fastened a powerful claw to what the local newspaper referred to as, 'a delicate part of the suspect's anatomy.'

"The suspect was taken to the hospital where a doctor was able to remove the tenacious lobster with pliers. After removing the lobster, the doctor said the patient should eventually recover.

"According to my friend, the store manager declined to press charges, saying that the shoplifter had probably learned a lesson and wouldn't be stealing any more lobsters."

Thanks for the email, Carol. I'm surprised you didn't add that—as a goodwill gesture—the lobster charged for the vasectomy.

You had me going for a while, Carol, but you began to lose me toward the end, there.

Since it happened in a small town like Bar Harbor I don't know if your imaginative story would qualify as an 'urban' legend. And when you step back and analyze your anecdote you see that it has a few problems.

For starters, although I don't shoplift, I assume that taking two live lobsters out of a huge water tank in the middle of a store and stuffing them down your pants isn't like slipping a pack of gum in your pocket. Someone would probably notice a move like that.

And, don't all lobsters that come to market have strong bands around their claws?

Over the years I've received dozens of letters asking about the Maine story of the bricklayer working on the lighthouse.

This bricklayer gets a letter from his insurance company asking him for additional information on the cause of his accident. He originally wrote simply, "poor planning."

In his response, he explains how he'd been attempting to lower a flat of unused bricks from the top of the scaffolding to the ground, using a rope and pulley.

When he untied the rope at ground level the weight of the bricks lifted him into the air, where he met the flat of bricks on its way to the ground—"This explains my fractured skull and broken collarbone," he relates.

He was hoisted to the top of the scaffolding where, "the fingers of my right hand were two knuckles deep in the pulley," but he managed to hold on to the rope.

When the flat of bricks hit the ground and the bricks fell off, the bricklayer was now too heavy. He began falling to the ground—eventually meeting the demolished flat, which, of course, was on its way up.

The encounter with the flat slowed him enough so that when he landed on the pile of bricks, "fortunately, only three vertebrae were cracked."

As he lay there in pain on top of the pile of bricks— unable to stand and watching the flat sixty feet above him— he let go of the rope.

Rick in Oxford writes: *"The other day, a bunch of us were sitting around on shore filleting some fish we had just caught in Thompson Lake and as we were cutting away, we got to wondering out loud about the jackknife and how it got its name. We know where the bowie knife got its name—from Jim Bowie. Any ideas on the jackknife, John?"*

Thanks for the letter, Rick. You write that you were filleting fresh-caught fish and talking about jackknifes, but you don't say whether you were using jackknifes to fillet your fish. It's just that I have enough trouble filleting fish with a fillet knife, so I don't think I'd ever approach the task with a jackknife. But that's a topic for another time.

Like you said, Rick, most everyone knows that the menacing-looking Bowie knife was named after its supposed inventor, the larger-than-life Jim Bowie, who was born in Kentucky, became a colonel in the U.S. Army, fought in the Texas Revolution, and died at the Alamo in 1836 at the age of 40.

People know even less about the invention of the handy jackknife, and if there was really a Jack involved in its creation.

And whoever this Jack is, Rick, he's managed to hang that name of his on a lot of things—Jack Frost, jack-of-all-trades, jack-in-the-box, jack boots, jackhammer, jackass and jackrabbit, to name but a few.

Some say the jackknife is named for King James I of England, who reigned from 1603 to 1625 and whose nickname was Jack (although few of his subjects called him that to his face). Because the jackknife was popular in England at the time of his reign, some historians think he is the Jack in the knife's name.

Then, just to be different, there's another group of historians who insist that the jackknife is named for its Belgian inventor—Jacques de Liege.

A Moose and a Lobster Walk into a Bar . . .

Dick from Windham writes: *"Hi, John. I'm writing in response to your discussion about the origins of the words 'port' and 'starboard'.*

"They did come from those pointy boats that you wrote about earlier. As you know (I assume), when they built boats many years ago, they had what we refer to as bows on both ends. To steer these boats, they had an early version of a rudder that was a board—sort of like an oar—that stuck out on the right, or the steer-board side.

"You can guess what would happen if your boat came up to a dock with this steer-board sticking out—so boats always came in to the dock on the left side, which became known as the 'port' side. I just thought you might like to have this useless piece of information."

Thanks for the email, Dick. Now all we need is a refresher course on spars, halyards, capstans and forecastles, which for some reason we're supposed to pronounce "folksle."

And, while we're on the subject, do they steer large vessels from the bridge, the pilothouse or the wheelhouse?

Gary from Palmyra writes: *"John, I heard this story down at the store here in town, and the fella who told it looked me right in the eye and assured me it was true.*

"A waitress in Bar Harbor found a wallet in her restaurant containing over $1,000 cash. This guy at the store said it took her a few days, but this waitress eventually tracked down the owner of the wallet, who was grateful for its return and went on about how he couldn't thank her enough.

"But rather than show his gratitude with a handsome reward, he merely gave her the $1 Megabucks ticket he happened to have with him.

"The waitress was so upset by the cheap gesture that she almost threw the ticket back at the fella, but she shoved it in her coat pocket instead and went on her way.

"The next Saturday, the ticket's numbers came up and the lucky waitress collected $3.5 million.

"Any truth to that story, John? Like I said, the fella here at the store claims it's true."

Thanks for the letter, Gary. I can understand why you'd tend to believe a story like that, since you heard it from some fella down at the store, which would almost guarantee its veracity.

Every morning in Maine some of the wisest scholars, pundits, poets, philosophers, and parolees gather in stores like yours, Gary, and tell one credible story after another. According to the state agency that regulates such activity— the Department of Veracity in Stores (DVS)—there has never been a falsehood uttered around a local store's coffee urns in the twenty-seven-year history of the agency.

I'd hate to think that the first falsehood was uttered in a nice town like Palmyra, Gary, but as far as I can tell, the story is bogus.

A good one, though.

Terry from Pownal writes: *"John, I've just returned from another delightful trip to Canada. Every time I visit our neighbors to the north I am reminded once again that America is one of the few countries in the civilized world that refuses to adapt to the metric system. What is it with us Americans and our fascination with things like the mile and the quart? Do you think we will ever go metric? And while we're talking about miles, why isn't the so-called nautical mile or knot the same as the land mile? I never could figure that one out."*

Thanks for your letter, Terry. It's funny that you mention our fascination with the mile and the quart because whenever I drive by one of those mileage signs on the turnpike that give me the distance to an exit in miles *and* kilometers, and every time I reach for a half-gallon of milk in the cooler at the grocery store, I feel kinda proud of the fact that America remains unique among all the nations of the world—so why shouldn't America have its own unique way of measuring things?

I know, Terry, that to the casual observer—or even the stiff, formal onlooker—our mile seems pretty arbitrary. Why 5,280 feet? Why not 5,250 feet? Or, better yet, 5,000 feet even?

When you look into the word *mile* and its origin, however, things start to become a little clearer. The first thing you learn is that the word mile has some relationship to that metric system you seem to be so fond of, Terry. Mile comes from the Latin word *mille*, which means one thousand. Your beloved kilometer comes from a Greek word that means the same thing. So, you see, the two systems start off with that much in common.

Long ago, when they were just beginning what would eventually become a vast, sprawling empire, the Romans wanted a standard unit of measure to keep track of things. They figured they had to know how big their empire was from one day to the next. After what we can only assume was lengthy and heated debate, they settled on something called the mille, or the distance a Roman foot soldier could cover in 1,000 paces. Turns out it was about 5,000 feet. I know it sounds like a stretch to say that someone, even a foot soldier, could go 5,000 feet in 1,000 paces, but that's what the Romans claimed.

Anyway, for hundreds of years, everyone agreed that the mille was 5,000 feet, and everything was just dandy in the Roman Empire, at least as far as measuring distances was concerned.

Trouble started brewing when the Romans introduced their popular mille to their newly conquered province, Briton. The Brits let the Romans know right off that they already had an equally popular standard of measure, thank you very much. The Brits used something called the furlong—and they were in no mood to change it just because the Romans had come along and conquered their beautiful island.

The well-liked furlong had been used in Briton to measure the length of a farmer's field and, I suppose, any other distance that needed measuring. The word came from two fine Old English words—furrow and length—and one furlong measured 660 feet.

As often happens in the course of human events, the two units of measure—the mille and the furlong—were blended together, and when all the dust had settled, it was decided that the mille (now known as the mile) would represent a distance equal to eight furlongs. Do the math, Terry, and you will discover that it comes out to 5,280 feet.

The whole business with the nautical mile, however, is quite different. First off, the nautical mile has nothing to do with either the paces of Roman foot soldiers or the contrary nature of British farmers, so it's not surprising to learn that the nautical mile is not 5,280 feet.

Only at sea is the mile 6,080 feet, or 1.15 land miles. But even here, Terry, the nautical mile had a metric history to it. Originally, the nautical mile was supposed to be 1,000 fathoms. For the landlubbers in the audience, a fathom is six feet, and was supposed to represent the length of a sailor's out-stretched arms. Once again, if you do the math, you might conclude that a nautical mile should be 6,000 feet, but, you'd be wrong.

How did the nautical mile go from 6,000 feet to 6,080 feet? Could be that the sailor they used to measure a fathom had a longer reach than most sailors. Who knows?

And, like many people, Terry, you seem to be confused by the words nautical mile and knot. A nautical mile is a measure of distance, and a knot is the measure of a ship's speed.

Don't ask me how it works, Terry, but in the early days of sailing, a ship's rate of speed was somehow measured by a log line marked off by pieces of cloth or knotted string.

Tom from Buffalo writes: *"John, we're buying a piece of property here in Maine and we're curious about the deed. It says the property line begins at a point, but isn't all that clear where the point is, and we can't find points of any kind anywhere on the land. The deed then concludes by saying the land contains 12.7 acres, more or less. Why is our Maine deed so vague, John?"*

Thanks for the letter, Tom. First of all, you shouldn't be too concerned about the point mentioned in your deed. If it ever existed, it's probably long gone, so forget about it. Just assume that the 12.7 acres mentioned in the deed is somewhere in the general vicinity of where the real estate agent said it was and operate accordingly. Your abutting neighbors will more or less do the same thing. When it comes to property lines here in Maine, it's always best to talk in vague generalities.

As for the "more or less" comment in your deed, I can understand your confusion. You probably already know that in the rest of the country—like your hometown of Buffalo, for instance—an acre is 43,560 square feet of land. Here in Maine, we view such foolish numbers as some out-a-state lawyer's clever idea. Down East, where there's plenty of land, folks are pretty arbitrary about things like acreage and such.

They tell about a man who wanted to divide his farm between his two sons. He sat at his kitchen table drawing a map, and then got up and started pacing off the boundary from the edge of the kitchen table—that was the point in his particular deed. He then went right out the kitchen door to a large oak tree in his pasture, and that line became the sons' boundary.

Everything went fine until one day someone moved the kitchen table and then a storm brought down the oak tree. The family's been feuding over that line ever since.

A Moose and a Lobster Walk into a Bar . . .

Sally from Indiana writes: *"John, what can you tell us about the Maine lobster?"*

Well, Sally, I can tell you it is known in scientific circles as Homarus *americanus* (which we think is Latin for humorous American). We can only guess that scientists called the lobster that because, as sophisticated Europeans, they thought it was pretty funny—or humorous—that anyone in their right mind, like Americans—or americanus—would even think of eating such an unappetizing-looking creature. Mainers know, however, that the homely looking lobster can easily hold its own against the tastiest foods on the planet, even those handsome snails and sturgeon eggs Europeans are always eating.

It makes little difference, Sally, whether you serve your lobster (or humorous American) boiled, baked, stuffed or stewed, saladed or newburged, you'll find your lobster makes mighty good eating.

And, Sally, if you ship any lobsters to friends in Indiana, make sure you tell them that live lobsters are not supposed to be red. It brings tears to my eyes to think of all the live lobsters that are shipped out of Maine to the Midwest and elsewhere to people who have never seen a live Maine lobster. When the lovely creatures arrive, the people think they are dead or diseased because they don't have a nice bright red color to them. So, they throw them all out.

CHAPTER SIX

I Remember . . .

Back home we had a neighbor—Sarah Phinney—who earned her living digging clams. This, of course, was years ago when there were still more than enough clams in Maine to go around. In good weather Sarah often dug two tides a day. She wasn't getting rich, but like most Mainers she was getting by. Her small house on the water was paid for, she always kept a large garden every summer, and her son managed to get a deer every fall. Sarah would tell anyone who asked that she was doing just fine, thank you.

Then one summer the coast of Maine was hit by one of the most severe cases of red tide in anyone's memory. Several hundred miles of rich clam flats were closed to shellfish harvesting. It got so bad that our senators and congressmen down there in Washington heard about it and went right to work. They eventually managed to shake loose a few million dollars from some government coffer, and the feds even opened offices in strategic towns to hand out what the clammers called "red tide checks."

I read all about the program, so the next time I saw Sarah we got to talking about this and that and eventually I asked her if she had been down to town hall to sign up for her red tide check.

"Not me," she said. "You won't catch me near that place."

"Why not?" I asked, a little confused. I figured if the red tide checks were intended to help anyone, they were intended to help someone like Sarah Phinney, who depended almost entirely on the cash she got from clam digging.

"You won't catch me going near that government crowd down there at the town hall, because once they get you to sign up for those checks, then they've got ya right where they want ya."

"What do you mean?" I asked.

"Think about it," she said. "If I go down there to the town hall and sign up for those special red tide checks, those folks'll write it all down and then they'll ask me all kinds of questions, like, 'So, Sarah, how much income are you losing by not being able to go clamming during this red tide tragedy?' And if I was foolish enough to tell them, then they'd say something like, 'Well, now, Sarah, if you've been earning that much income over the years clamming, how come the Internal Revenue Service has no record that you've ever reported that income on your tax forms?'"

"You're probably right," I said.

Now, I don't want to say anything one way or the other about Sarah's tax situation, or her status with the IRS, and I certainly don't endorse withholding tax information from the proper authorities. But over the years, I've often had occasion to think of Sarah's comments, and how complicated our lives have become.

I thought about Sarah, a rugged Down East individualist, again the other day when I read about the folks from the Federal Emergency Management Agency (FEMA), who were seeking applications from people who suffered losses during the recent ice storm here in Maine. I know that the storm did a lot of serious damage and a lot of people were hurt financially. Those people really do need help.

I've heard that the federal government has programs to pay for things like the electric generator you bought (as long as you can prove that you bought that generator while your power was still off).

They say other programs give you emergency housing, if necessary, and still other programs will help people who missed work. There are also federal programs to provide you with grants or low-cost loans. But before you go and sign up for one program or another, you might want to pause and remember the words of that true Mainer, Sarah Phinney, who made it clear that she wanted nothing to do with the red tide checks of so many years ago.

"Once they get you to sign up, then they've got ya right where they want ya."

Around mid-March each year as I drive through rural Maine and New Hampshire, I start seeing those bright silver sap buckets on hundreds of sugar maple trees. And almost every year as I drive along past the buckets and the trees, I start to think: "This spring, why don't I make myself some of that maple syrup? What could be so difficult about tapping those maples on our back line along the brook? All I'd have to do is take a little metal spout and tap it into the sugar maple tree; then take a clean bucket and hang it on a hook under the spout. Before long—like magic—the sweet sap begins to flow."

A Moose and a Lobster Walk into a Bar...

In my head, it all sounds simple enough. All I'd have to do is pour my sap into a pretty good-sized pan on the woodstove, boil the sap down and—Voila!—all the delicious maple syrup I could ask for. There'd be more than enough for our pancakes and waffles and ice cream and anything else we'd want to pour the sweet stuff on. And the best part is, I'd hardly have to do a thing. The maple tree and the wood-stove do all the work. I'd just sit there. While the sap is boiling, I could eat bonbons and watch *Oprah*.

By the way, it also hadn't escaped my notice that this pure maple syrup—that could be made so easily right there in your kitchen while watching your favorite day-time show—sells in stores for ten to twelve dollars a quart! It seemed like having a license to print money. The only thing that didn't make sense was why up there in maple tree country, you don't see more people driving around in those expensive BMWs and Mercedes and large SUVs. You're more likely to see a Ford or Chevy or Dodge pickup parked in the driveway of a maple syrup tycoon.

But back to my original thought.

One year I decided to do more than just think about how easy it would be to make a small fortune in the maple syrup industry. I decided to go out and do something about it. After all, why should these moguls of the maple groves, these sheiks of the syrup cartel here in rural New England, be making all this easy money off saps like the rest us? (No pun intended.)

The next morning, I went down to my local cooperative extension office here in South Paris to find out how I could get into the maple syrup business. The friendly folks there in the office loaded me up with all kinds of reading material on the wonderful world of sap.

After doing some reading, I tried to contact some maple syrup kingpins to talk to them about the sap business. It surprised me at first to discover that most of these maple syrup makers weren't in their houses eating bonbons and watching *Oprah* as their sap boiled on the stove. I discovered that most maple sugar folks have full-time jobs and only work their maple sugar operations early in the morning before going to work and in the evening when they get home. And it shocked me further to learn that the ten to twelve dollars a quart they get for their pure maple syrup isn't pure profit. But I wasn't deterred. I was more determined than ever to try it.

I went down to my local hardware store and loaded up on spouts and buckets and came home to start tapping some maples.

Early the next morning I awoke, and I couldn't wait to get out there by the brook to check my sap buckets so I could start boiling sap to make some syrup. I built a roaring fire in the woodstove and then went outside to check my buckets. The first two buckets were pretty nigh full, which was good. But while carrying the two buckets back to the house, I spilled a good part of the sap into my rubber boots, which wasn't too good. One of the buckets I came to that first morning had a dead mouse in it. Also not good.

"Would this dead mouse give the sap a 'funny' taste?" I wondered to myself. Not wanting to experiment with such things at this fledgling stage of my pending tycoon-dom, I decided to dump out the mouse and the sap it was floating in. That first morning, I managed to get close to twelve gallons of sap, and it only took me about a cord of wood and a day or so to boil it down on the stove. The family wasn't too pleased that the kitchen felt like a Swedish sauna all the while it was boiling. "That's life in the sap lane," I told them. They were not amused.

From that twelve gallons of sap, I managed to get me a little over one quart of maple syrup. And considering what I went through in time and material to get it, if you think I'd sell that precious quart for less than $200, you're crazy!

Any day now, I plan to start work on my second quart.

Although I watch birds at the feeders just outside our kitchen window, I wouldn't call myself a birdwatcher. To me, a birdwatcher is a very serious person (or at least someone a lot more serious than me) who takes well-organized trips with groups of other serious birdwatchers. They load up their late model sports utility vehicles and head into the woods and fields toting bags filled with expensive binoculars and cameras and lots of other birdwatching equipment. These serious people spend days at a time—whole vacations, even—doing nothing but looking for all kinds of different birds. That is not what I do.

When I'm in the kitchen, I'll often look out the window and see what birds are hanging around the feeders. And then I'll go on to something else.

Like most things, this whole business with the birds started innocently enough. Soon after we moved to our present home here in the beautiful Oxford Hills area, my wife and I noticed that there didn't seem to be many birds around our yard. A while later, someone happened to give us a suet feeder as a gift. Since suet isn't among the essential food groups, we didn't have any lying around the house. And since we weren't in the habit of buying suet, the feeder sat on a shelf for quite some time. One day when I was in a local hardware store I happened to buy a cake of suet and eventually I hung the suet feeder on a tree by the kitchen window. Well, that feeder could have been hanging on the moon for all the attention it got at first. Not a single bird or bird-like creature came near the thing. For weeks it hung there, swinging in the breeze.

After what seemed like months, a stray bird, a nuthatch, happened by the suet feeder for a visit. One minute this suet feeder was hanging there unused, and the next minute, here's this solitary, wandering nuthatch chowing down at it. I'll admit it was an event. A few days later, the lone nuthatch returned for more suet. Over the next few months small bands of chickadees and individual woodpeckers joined the nuthatch, and our feeder was finally in business. But business was definitely slow.

Not wanting to go overboard with this bird feeding business we left just the one suet feeder hanging there on the tree by the kitchen window for over a year. Birds were so few and far between that that first suet cake seemed to last forever.

One morning in the fall, while preparing things for winter, I was again in my local hardware store and on a whim, I picked up a deluxe, clear plastic, triple-decker, multi-seed bird feeder, just for the heck of it. That afternoon I hung the fancy new feeder on the tree by the suet feeder.

The fancy feeder got a little more attention—mostly from chickadees—but business was still slow. Winter arrived and the snow began to pile up. This time when the ground was covered, the feeders got busier.

This spring, as warm weather approached, our feeders actually got real busy. There are now times when we almost need an air-traffic controller in the backyard. We've even had to get another feeder. Now there are chickadees, nuthatches, woodpeckers, and all kinds of finches out there all hours of the day. Bluebirds show up in groups and try to feed, as do starlings.

The chickadees are like the native Mainers who stick it out through the long cold winter. I now spend a lot of time watching those birds, but I'm no birdwatcher.

As a kid, I always had mixed feelings about what I considered "adult" holidays—like Thanksgiving. Unlike the huge children's days—Halloween and Christmas—Thanksgiving involved a lot of adult activities like dressing up in Sunday best and greeting lots of older relatives and being banished to kids' tables in the kitchen. It meant dealing with foods like boiled onions and yams and huge serving dishes of turnip. Sure, Christmas involved a lot of those very same things, but Christmas also had piles and piles of presents to make up for an awful lot of yams and boiled onions.

Thanksgiving held out no promise of presents or special candy. All it did was serve as a reminder to children everywhere that Christmas was still a lengthy four weeks away. And it's a good bet that the ones who dreamed up the Thanksgiving menu didn't have youngsters in mind.

At my Thanksgivings in the 1950s and 60s, relatives would start arriving sometime around mid-morning, toting all kinds of strange foods. There seemed to be almost no rules. Aunts from up the coast brought things like herring, haddock, boiled salt mackerel and cold glazed salmon. Some years, we had relatives venture in from Penobscot Bay islands bearing creamed finnan haddie and baked cod or flounder. Other aunts from upcountry brought all kinds of relishes and lots of pickled things—including spouses.

No matter who brought what, you could always count on Aunt Gertrude to bring along some of the most peculiar items on the menu—pickled watermelon rinds, rhubarb relish, pickled onions, pickled string beans, red cabbage, green tomatoes, pickled herring, something called chow chow and winter chili sauce. It was almost as if Aunt Gertrude had taken everything in her garden, chopped it up and threw it into a vat of vinegar.

As a youngster, it was always a bit astonishing to me to see how many of the old folks would load up on Aunt Gertrude's scary relishes as they made several successful rounds of the crowded dinner table on fancy cut glass relish trays.

Even now, so many years later, I get a little queasy just thinking about all that food.

Thanksgiving tables never included—and probably never will include—items for the kids. We never had macaroni and cheese, or hot dogs, or potato chips, or peanut butter. Even in those days, I knew that the best part of Thanksgiving was the leftovers that would follow for days afterward—but it seemed like a lot of trouble to endure just to get those terrific turkey sandwiches.

As I grew older, I realized that Thanksgiving was not a total loss. I liked a lot of the relatives who came to visit; and

A Moose and a Lobster Walk into a Bar . . .

I liked the excitement and sense of anticipation that filled
the house from one end to the other. When you got that
many different relatives together in one house at one time,
you never knew what might happen when touchy subjects
like politics or religion came up—as they always did.

Once the dinner was over and the dishes were done, most
everybody gathered in the double front parlor for songs and
stories.

My Uncle Abner would often start the stories by telling
about Thanksgivings gone by. He had been born in the
late nineteenth century, and raised in a house less than half
a mile from where we all sat. He had gone to a one-room
schoolhouse just down the street, and at fourteen, he went
to sea on a schooner named the *Volunteer* out of Searsport. I
never tired of his stories about those days.

Uncle Abner would tell of the holidays when he was
at sea or in some foreign port. He would tell of fierce
November storms and Thanksgiving shipwrecks.

Those who didn't want to hang around and listen, and
didn't mind the blustery winds, would go for long walks.
Other folks would just sit around digesting. But most of us
would sit and while away the hours listening to stories.

These days, my Thanksgivings don't include servings of
pickled herring or creamed finnan haddie, and I don't mind
one bit. But I sure do miss those stories.

You can't pick up a newspaper or magazine these days
without being forced to read something about the new
television season. Myself, I'd prefer to sit and read a good
Annual Town Report than subject myself to some of the
new shows they're dragging out these days on television.
Your average town report can be a lot more original, sus-
penseful and humorous than your average new TV show.

I was born into a family that didn't own a television set.
We had all kinds of radios and lots of stories to entertain
each other, but no television. Now before you start assum-
ing that I must have come from the wrong side of town and
was deprived as a child, let me assure you that nothing of
the kind was the case. Fact is, our town didn't have a wrong
side, as far as I know. And as for being deprived—my father
was a dentist with a successful practice and there wasn't a
whole lot that we lacked.

In those days, no one in our town had a television much
before the mid-fifties, which is about the time we finally
bought ours. However, some of my fondest early childhood
memories are of lying on the floor in the front room listening to programs on our enormous radio, easily as big as a
refrigerator. My father was probably sitting in his easy chair
reading a good town report.

The biggest problem people had with television in those
days was what we used to call "reception." We lived so far
upcountry that you needed more than a set of rabbit ears on
the top of your set to get anything.

Sherm Ames was the first person in our little town with a
television. He was a clever handyman with all kinds of fancy
tools and he looked upon the tricky business of television
reception as just another challenge.

A Moose and a Lobster Walk into a Bar . . .

Around about 1953, Sherm decided to get himself a television, and so he built himself a huge tower there beside his house with a large TV antenna on top of it. Sherm figured if he was going to have one of these newfangled televisions he was going to have the best reception in the county. That tower rig of Sherm's had the cleverest remote control mechanism you ever saw. It allowed Sherm to spin that antenna in any direction he wanted—and he could do it all from the comfort of his recliner there in his parlor. Once he got the whole rig set up and running he hardly ever watched it, but Sherm, a true Down Easter, just wanted to have that television ready for when he had a mind to watch it.

Most nights Sherm would check to see what stations his set was pulling in even if he had no plans to watch. He would routinely get stations from Portland and Bangor and occasionally Boston. Some nights, if conditions were just right, Sherm could get stations from Providence or New Haven. On those rare nights he'd make a point of coming up to our house to brag a little about how great his reception was. He'd also say that if we wanted to, we could come down and watch some television with him and Thelma, his wife. Even after we got our television, we'd often stop by to watch Sherm's set just because he got so many different stations and his reception was so clear.

Kids today have no idea how hard life was in those early days of television when we'd stand around the schoolyard and talk about things like our television reception.

Life in the fifties was pretty rough, what with only one or two television channels to watch at any one time. In the sixties, when people in town eventually had three or four stations to choose from, they'd still complain that despite the expanded choices, there still wasn't anything on television worth watching.

I thought of Sherm Ames the other day as I sat surfing the channels on my cable service, finding nothing worth watching. And I don't have the limited cable package, either, meaning limited to those stations I could otherwise get free over the air. I have a slightly expanded cable package in which the cable company generously throws in (another story, for another day) a bunch of shopping channels, a bowling channel, an archery channel and the psycho-friends network for a paltry $26.90 per month.

Of course, for real money, I could have a movie package clogged with movie channels showing numb movies they couldn't get people to go see in the theaters.

If Sherm were still around I don't think he'd waste much time with cable. He'd have himself a huge satellite rig and would be pulling in stuff from around the world. And once he got finished building it, he still wouldn't watch it. He'd be too busy making something else out in his shop. Besides, there'd still be nothing to watch, anyway.

I am the proud son of a country dentist. My father, T. Way McDonald, graduated from Tufts Dental School in 1939 and practiced dentistry Down East and elsewhere for fifty years—retiring in 1989. I don't know why they call it "practicing dentistry." I always thought he had the business of dentistry down pretty well, and as I recall, he was quite good at it.

A Moose and a Lobster Walk into a Bar . . .

Like most dentists Down East my father had to be flexible and creative when it came to getting people to pay for their dental work. A fella with a toothache was usually an easy customer. Someone suffering with a bad toothache would most often have the good sense to bring the cash for having it pulled right in his pocket. My father would pull the tooth and the fella would reach in his pocket and take out the required fee.

For other procedures, it was well known for miles around that my father would take everything from land to lobsters in trade for his professional services.

We lived right there in the middle of town in a big old house, and my father's office took up a part of the first floor. Because the house was so big and so old, my father was always looking for ways to trade out dental work for carpentry work, or masonry work, or electrical work, or firewood or lawn care. Having a large family to feed, he would also take a side of beef, a bunch of hens or a pile of vegetables in trade as well.

One time—back in 1964—a little old lady came to my father's office and said she finally decided to get herself a full set of upper and lower false teeth but she had one problem: "I don't have enough cash to pay for new teeth."

"That's no problem here," my father said, almost out of habit. "What do you have to trade for some teeth?"

"I've got that pretty little 1953 Chevy sitting out there in your parking lot," she answered.

My father walked over to the window to look at the car and thought that the little Chevy looked almost as good as new.

When he asked her why she would give up such a nice car just to get a set of false teeth, the woman said, "I find I'm using that car less and less all the time, but I need teeth as much as ever. So I'd be willing to trade that car for some nice new choppers."

My father agreed to the trade—a pretty little car for a set of pretty teeth—and began taking impressions of the women's teeth. (One of the few bumper stickers my father ever allowed on any of his cars was the one that said: "Dentists always make a good impression.")

I was never too concerned about those false teeth, but I sure would like to know what happened to that old 1953 Chevy.

When my Uncle Abner died, father traded out some of the cost of the undertaker for some nice expensive dental work. Doug Campbell, the undertaker, was well respected in town for making his customers look so good at their funerals. But I tell you, by the time my father got through fixing up his mouth, that undertaker was smiling more than he'd ever done in his life. He was so proud of his fancy new crowns that he had all he could do to keep a straight face at his funerals, which almost ruined his reputation as a serious undertaker.

When my sisters got married, my father would always call a fella in town who rented those large, fancy canopies. The fella would trade the canopy for dental work. And it wouldn't stop there. Father would trade with the caterer, the florist—even members of the band.

My father always admired the classic Maine lobster boat, so when he decided to get himself a boat for cruising the coast, he went to a boatyard up there in Stonington to order himself one. A quick walk through the boatyard convinced my father that there was more than enough dental work needed to get himself a boat. All he had to do was talk the boatbuilders into doing some trading.

To this day, I wish my father had actually done it. I know he could have managed to work a deal with the yard for dental work and some cash in exchange for a beautiful 38-foot boat with twin Chrysler Crown Marine engines. At the boat launching, folks would have said they never saw so many wide, toothy smiles on a crew of boatbuilders in their lives.

Let's just face it: In Maine, we're never really that far from the cold weather. To make sure we understand what that means, Nature sees to it that some of the leaves on some of our best maple trees start turning bright red in the middle of summer—long before you'd expect them to, or want them to. Nature has these maples pull this stunt not just to show that trees can be as contrary as any other living thing here in Maine, but because Nature doesn't want us Mainers to get too comfy with the few days of warm weather in July and August that are so unnatural to our state.

How many times have you been driving along a country road in July when you come around a curve and there they are—the suddenly bright red or purple leaves of a maple tree. You try to turn your eyes away, but it's too late. You've seen them, and as a Mainer you know their meaning. As you continue driving along you start thinking of the cool fall days that are just down the road, so to speak.

Before you know it, you stop thinking about the barbecue you're planning for the weekend with friends and neighbors, and you start thinking of the cars and buses filled with fall tourists that will soon be heading up the turnpike. Those people, known as "leaf peepers or "leafers," will drive along our roads looking with wonder at all the colorful leaves.

When I was a kid, I'd often go down the road and visit my Uncle Abner and see if there was anything I could do to help him around his place. Even as a kid I couldn't quite understand why doing work at someone else's place was always more fun than doing the same work around your own place, but it was. On those warm summer days more often than not Uncle Abner was getting his place ready for the cooler weather that was just around the corner. He warned us: "Oh, it's a gorgeous day today, but days are gettin' shorter. Cold weather'll be here before long."

It really annoyed me when Uncle Abner talked like that. On those glorious summer days of my youth, the last thing I wanted to hear about was how short the days were getting and how soon the cold weather—and school days—would return.

Often Uncle Abner would be in the barn cutting firewood with his giant buck saw. If he wasn't cutting the wood, he was splitting it and stacking it against the barn's back wall. On those hot summer days long ago, Uncle Abner—at some point—would pause from his work, mop his brow and say something like: "He warms himself twice who cuts his own wood." If I heard him say that once, I bet I heard him say it a thousand times.

After a while Aunt Lydia would come through the door with a welcome pitcher of lemonade and a plate of sugar cookies. Even now, when I hear the delicate sound of ice cubes gently rattling in a glass pitcher I think of those times.

I'd see the refreshments coming, and Uncle Abner would decide it was time for a break. We'd then sit in the shade in wooden lawn chairs, drink the lemonade, and eat Aunt Lydia's cookies. Before long the stories would start. Oh, I knew most of them by then, but I'd always sit and listen.

A Moose and a Lobster Walk into a Bar . . .

Uncle Abner went to sea at the age of fourteen and during our breaks, he enjoyed telling about the summer days of his youth when they'd sail up the Kennebec to Hallowell to take on a load of ice. As they waited at the dock for the ice to be loaded, he would take in all the activity along the waterfront.

One time when they were tied along the dock waiting for the ice to be loaded, he looked across the street to an empty lot and noticed two men in the hot sun furiously digging in the sand. "What are those men up to?" he asked one of the crew members.

Another crewman said, "Oh, them fellas? They're probably digging for groundhogs. If you get a nice fat one and cook it up right, they make awful good eating."

Uncle Abner said that over the years he'd offered to bring one home to Aunt Lydia to cook, but she'd say, "Don't you dare! I won't touch one."

When Uncle Abner retired from the sea, he went into real estate. He was considered quite an expert on Maine land and people would often come to him for advice.

Uncle Abner would say you should always look at land in the middle of March—not some beautiful July or August day.

He'd say: "Any place in Maine that looks decent in March has got to be a nice piece of property. You should never go looking at real estate in the summah."

"Why's that? people would ask.

"Summah in Maine is so beautiful that it's pretty hard for any house to look bad," he would answer.

And, of course, it was summer and it was time to get ready for winter because the days were getting shorter.

In an oft-quoted poem, Robert Frost wrote about "the road not taken." In our town, folks were more familiar with the roads not paved.

I grew up back in the 1950s in a town that had as many dirt roads as tarred roads. My family's road—Hart's Neck Road—was tarred down to a little past our driveway, and then it was dirt for another few miles until it just ended at the Aldridge place.

When I started driving cars, at about twelve, I could go for miles on the back roads all around our house. For almost two years, I drove on those roads before I ever met a car coming the other way. I was never the least bit concerned about there not being enough room on those small country roads for the car I was driving, but the first time I saw another car approach I began to sweat buckshot wondering how we were going to get those two cars past each other in one piece.

The roads were pretty narrow and rustic and everyone knew that nature could take the whole road back almost any time it wanted to.

So the roads had to be tended to and fussed with every now and then. Every few years in the summertime the town's crack road crew would come around and pour a thick layer of hot, black tar over the old road, and then they'd bring in truckloads of gravel and spread it over the whole gooey mess. The idea was to have the tires on the cars press the two ingredients together. Pretty basic stuff.

The first time my father took us for a ride on the new Maine Turnpike, I just couldn't believe that such a fine smooth road existed anywhere in Maine. Oh, sure, there were moose here and there to dodge, but the turnpike itself was just like velvet.

A Moose and a Lobster Walk into a Bar . . .

I also remember that in school in the fifties we used to get the *Weekly Reader* that would tell us a little about what was going on in the world beyond our town. There was a section each week that told about what things would be like in the future when we grew up.

One week, there was an article about roads of the future. It said that some scientists were quite certain that in the future we would all ride around on electronic roads and that our cars would be able to drive along on these high-tech wonders—automatically. Next to the incredible story was an even more implausible picture—an artist's idea of a typical family of the future wearing clothes of the future and sitting in a sleek futuristic looking car that was speeding along a beautiful futuristic highway with no one at the wheel—and not a moose in sight.

Considering the amount of arguing it took at our town meetings just to get a simple piece of road equipment, I couldn't imagine the day when these fancy futuristic cars would be tooling down an "electronic" Hart's Neck Road.

So, you can imagine my surprise when I picked up the newspaper the other day and began to read about the nation's first automated highway. It was déjà vu all over again.

According to the story—which seems as implausible now as it did years ago in the *Weekly Reader*—test vehicles equipped with video cameras, magnets and radar navigated down the nation's first 7.6 miles of experimental automated highway.

The story also said, "Tiny magnets embedded in the asphalt on either side of traffic lanes at four-foot intervals enable the magnetized vehicle to constantly orient itself within the lane's boundaries." Right.

The article never even mentioned the old *Weekly Reader* piece from the fifties, but said the genesis was a 1991 federal law that empowered the Transportation Department to develop "fully automated, intelligent vehicle highway systems." I guess they've given up trying to develop intelligent drivers and now want to turn the whole process over to computers.

Call me old fashioned, but I'm just not ready to turn my car over to a bunch of magnets in the asphalt and a computer under the dash. I have enough trouble these days with the whole idea of ATMs and voice mail—and those things don't move anywhere near 60 mph.

No, I'd sooner trust the guys in our town's road crew to design a "fully automated, intelligent vehicle highway system," before I'd trust the transportation crowd down in Washington to design me one. First, because I'll be long gone before they ever get around to installing it; and second, if they ever did install it, at least here in town we could complain to selectmen if things didn't go right. How are you going to argue with a bunch of transportation folks in Washington? By voice mail?

Just the other day, I looked out the window at my bleak lawn where the first tough blades of grass are beginning to push through the brown patches and I realized how much I missed the kids. Oh, the wife and I miss our three grown children all the time, and talk to them often on the phone. But where my lawn is concerned, I began to realize—ever since they grew up and began moving out—that I miss them even more than usual come springtime.

A Moose and a Lobster Walk into a Bar . . .

When we had three healthy, active kids living around here I could blame the barren land around our house—where childless people had lush green lawns—on the fact that we had three growing kids. Add to that the fact that each kid had at least three friends and the whole pack of them had bikes and dogs and all those bikes and dogs seemed to be constantly rolling and running across the bleak landscape where something resembling a lawn might have been.

All that rolling and running was pretty rough on the yard—but it didn't stop there.

In summer, we'd always have to get at least one plastic pool, for those hot days when we couldn't get to our camp. And of course, there were the countless baseball games.

Come fall there was football, and in winter there were all of those sleds.

Each spring, after the snow finally melted, I'd look out the window at the desolate stretch of dirt that ran around our house and I'd dream of the lush, green lawn I'd have as soon as the kids were grown.

Occasionally—as I lay in my hammock listening to the Red Sox and sipping lemonade—I'd think about training the kids to fertilize, mow and trim the lawn so they could appreciate what it takes to maintain a yard. But I'd soon reconsider. Since we had no lawn to fertilize or mow in the first place, and since it would take at least two months of constant fussing to get one (and once we had one, the kids would no longer have a place to play), I'd soon dismiss the absurd idea and continue listening to the ballgame.

"Just wait until the kids are grown," I'd repeat to myself. "What a beautiful lawn you're going to have then, John."

My kids were also my best excuse for things like genteel poverty. Kids had to eat and all that food cost money. Kids needed clothes and school supplies and pets and orthodontists and music lessons and trips to Disney World. And every one of those necessities cost money—money those sad, childless couples used to go scuba diving in the Caribbean.

Oh, sure, there were some expenses back then that, like any father, I'd question.

Some mornings I'd walk into the upstairs bathroom, after one of the kids had just taken a shower, and I'd be overcome by the steam. At those times I'd wonder aloud to the family why it took almost 40 minutes and hundreds of gallons of hot water to wash a 100-pound body when I could thoroughly clean one twice as large in under 10 minutes.

Every week our kids got something like $2 each for an allowance. But I couldn't hand over that kind of money to a kid without giving the required father's lecture on the value of money.

"When I was your age, I got 25 cents a week and with that I had to buy all my clothes, school lunches and books and take what was left over and put it in the bank for college."

There were the times I'd come home and find the whole house lit up like a Christmas tree. I'd then give the, "Do you think your poor father's made of money?" speech:

"You know, kids, when this house was built they went to great expense to put a light switch near the door to every room so that the light in the room can be turned off when it's not needed and money can be saved. Can we try to take advantage of these clever devices?"

I won't go into the business about the empty ice cube trays. I'm sure I filled thousands of ice cube trays over the years, and yet every time I opened the freezer compartment for a few ice cubes, the trays were always empty.

A Moose and a Lobster Walk into a Bar . . .

Well, the kids are now grown and gone and with them all my good excuses.

Now that those 40-minute showers are over we are a bit more prosperous, but we still have too many lights on, the ice trays are still empty and my pathetic excuse for a lawn remains.

And there's no one around to blame but me.

I have seen them over the years along the coast of Maine in the summertime, usually way out on the bay under full sail, gliding along silently and majestically. I've always wanted to board one to take a look and maybe go for a sail. I'm talking about those beautiful vessels of Maine's historic windjammer fleet. Like most of us here in Maine, I'd always assumed that windjammers were mostly for those summer-folks who drive up here to The Pine Tree State to do things like take bay cruises and river-rafting trips and such. I had never taken the time to go sailing on a windjammer myself, and didn't know many people who had. But, I'd always kept "take windjammer cruise" on my long list of things to do.

So you can imagine that I got pretty enthusiastic when Ken and Ellen Barnes, owners of the schooner *Stephen Taber*, the oldest documented sailing vessel in continuous service in the United States, invited me to join them aboard their fine vessel for a few days of sailing. In short order, I managed to clear my calendar, pack my sea bags and plan a trip to Rockland. However, as my departure date approached I started getting a tad anxious and wondered if I should postpone the trip.

You see, after all those years of thinking about windjammers, I began to worry that I would finally get out on one of those great vessels and get sick, or, worse, not enjoy it. I eventually came to my senses and managed to put such crazy thoughts out of my mind and pressed on with my plans to go sailing.

Most of the windjammers in the Rockland and Camden fleet leave port every Monday morning during the season. On most windjammers, folks booked for a week's cruise can board their vessel late Sunday afternoon and spend their first night in their cabin. So, on a recent Sunday morning after my radio show, I headed to Rockland to board the *Stephen Taber*.

Now, I've learned enough about boats over the years to know that I should probably keep my mouth shut when I'm around real boat experts. What was it Abraham Lincoln said? Something like: "It is better to remain silent and be thought a fool, than to open your mouth and remove all doubt." With that in mind, when I stepped aboard the *Stephen Taber*, I planned to do a lot of listening and little talking.

Don't get me wrong—I have learned quite a few nautical things over the years. I know more than most and don't need a helpful chart with arrows to explain things like the bow is the pointy end of the boat and the stern is the flat end. Over the years, I've learned other important things such as port and left each have four letters, so it's easy to remember that the port side of the boat is the left side. Also, port wine is red, and red running lights are on the port or left side of the boat, and red buoys should be kept on the right or starboard side when you're coming into port (or, even shorter, red, right, returning). And finally, I know, "Red skies at night are a sailors delight. Red skies at dawning, a sailor takes warning."

Anyway, I went aboard the *Stephen Taber* and had myself one heck of a time. In fact, I can't wait to go back to sea again. The *Stephen Taber* is a beautifully restored nine-teenth-century coasting schooner that is now equipped to handle over twenty passengers. Ken and Ellen Barnes and their top-notch crew worked hard to create for us passengers a unique sailing experience. As I stood on the deck there on that Monday morning and the *Stephen Taber* left port under full sail, all my land-bound troubles were left behind. We sailed off into a world of canvas and ropes and wind and charts and bells. We became more concerned with boat tillers than bank tellers and more intent on watching sails than on making sales.

Life is different on the water, and it changes you. When you first enter your cabin, you wonder how you'll survive in such a small space. In a few days you begin to wonder why you need all that space on land.

While we passengers sat comfortably on deck telling stories and watching the islands of Penobscot Bay go by, the crew went about the business of swabbing decks and polishing brass. At midday we all had steaming bowls of fish chowder and homemade bread on deck. It was as fine a time as any I've ever had here in Maine. By late afternoon on our first day out, we had arrived off Castine.

I don't have enough space here to tell you about the entire trip. We went from Smith Cove to Castine to Buck's Harbor to Stonington. It was a wonderful trip. Now when I see those magnificent vessels quietly gliding by way off at sea, instead of just dreaming, I'll start planning my next cruise.

After finishing college in the sixties, I decided not to head right back to Maine. Instead, I remained in exile in Rhode Island for a few years. The first job offered to me after graduation was that of cub reporter for the *Pawtucket Times*.

I was an English major—so what did I know? Not much. I knew all kinds of neat things about our Mother Tongue, like the exact moment that it went from Old English to Middle English (October 14, 1318, at around two in the afternoon). I also knew all about the famous "Diphthong Shift" that occurred in our language a few years later. But that's about all I knew. It wasn't the kind of knowledge that employers were screaming for in the job market of 1968.

In academic circles (and even some scholarly squares and triangles), they say that after graduation, the typical philosophy major continues to ask "Why?" The engineering major asks, "How does it work?" And your typical English major asks, "Would you like fries with that?'"

Not having studied any subjects even remotely related to journalism—or any other useful trade, for that matter—I was glad to get any job. I wasn't sure what a reporter did, but I soon learned.

Most of those early days at the *Times* were spent taking obits over the phone, or putting together the television listings, which included brief descriptions of shows and movies. I probably shouldn't admit this here in print, but to relieve the tedium of the job, I occasionally made up a movie or two and listed my friends as the stars. I would write something like: Chan. 4, 8 p.m. *Bright Nebraska Nights*, starring Tom Cavanaugh—the electrifying tale of an accountant from Fond du Lac, Wisconsin, who manages to find happiness as a cabaret singer in naughty Lincoln, Nebraska. Parental discretion advised."

A Moose and a Lobster Walk into a Bar . . .

After a few of these listings ran in the paper without any notice whatsoever, I realized that no one—not one single person—ever read the TV listings that I sweated over for hours. I never once heard a single word from editors or readers. Nothing.

Eventually I was taken off the obit and television desk and given my own beat to cover. I was named the *Times* reporter for the town of Seekonk, just over the state line in Massachusetts. Being an English major, I also knew that the word "Seekonk" was a fine example of onomatopoeia—where the word imitates the natural sound of the thing designated. Other examples would be crackle, roar and sizzle.

But I digress.

The most exciting story I ever covered in my distinguished career in Seekonk was a daring bank robbery at the Industrial National Bank. The robbery actually occurred while I was at the Seekonk police station looking for stories.

One morning, just after the bank opened, someone called and asked for the manager. The caller then told the manager, who had just moved to the area from a large city, that he was calling from the Seekonk Police Department. He said the police had just received a tip that the bank would be robbed that morning. The caller went on to say that police could do nothing until the person actually robbed the bank, but plainclothes officers would have the bank under surveillance and would nab the robber as soon as he came out to the parking lot. The bank manager thanked the officer and said he would inform his tellers.

A few minutes later a man wearing dark glasses walked into the bank and announced, "This is a robbery," and ordered the tellers to fill his large canvas bag. Coyly winking to each other, the tellers happily filled the bag with money. When they were finished the man quickly left.

The manager and tellers then ran to the front windows to watch the police move in. But there were no police in sight.

"Maybe they're going to nab him when he leaves the parking lot," the manager said a little nervously.

No nabbing was done.

You've probably already guessed that the bank robber was the original caller and the Seekonk police knew nothing about it.

So, John, what does this have to do with Maine? I hear some of you ask.

Good question.

A few weeks later, the robber repeated his clever M.O. here, but the Maine bank manager was not fooled. He knew everyone on the small town's police force. In fact, the force consisted of only one person—his brother-in-law Earl. And Earl nabbed the robber in the parking lot after the daring robbery.

After covering Seekonk for several years, the excitement became too much for me and I returned to Maine to work for the *Bangor Daily News* in their Ellsworth bureau.

I thought of all this last night when I noticed in the TV listings that the film *Bright Nebraska Nights* was going to be on at 8.

A Moose and a Lobster Walk into a Bar . . .

My Uncle Abner was born and raised on an island off the coast of Maine and didn't live on the mainland for any length of time until he started high school. One of the many chores he had on the island for several years was building a fire in the wood furnace of the school he attended every morning.

The colder it was outside, the longer it would take to get that schoolhouse to a decent temperature. So on bitter cold winter mornings, Uncle Abner would always make sure he was up an hour earlier so he could do his family chores and get down to the school in time to start the fire. Everyone just assumed that when it was time for classes to begin, the school would always be nice and toasty—and it was.

As the weather got warmer Uncle Abner didn't have to get up as early, and on some late spring mornings he didn't have to light a fire at all. The decision was his and he took the job seriously. He never got any memos from a central office and nobody ever had to remind him or check up on him. He just did it.

In fact, he did such a good job at the school that he was given the same job at the church. Every Sunday morning and Wednesday evening, he'd build a fire there, too. He said in the dead of winter he'd have to start a fire in the church wood furnace by six in order for it to be warm enough for the ten o'clock service.

Uncle Abner talked often of that small school on the island and the many important things he learned there. Years later, when Maine towns organized into School Administrative Districts (SADs) and started building large regional schools and busing students from great distances, Uncle Abner was concerned. He said the vast new schools would probably have all kinds of fancy gizmos like electric furnaces and thermostats and the poor kids would miss out on those important experiences he had as a kid—experiences like building a fire every morning in the wood furnace of his island school. I never said anything but, as a kid, I didn't agree.

Uncle Abner said the SAD (please note the acronym) system took several small towns that didn't get along all that well anyway and bound them together so they could raise enough money to build bigger schools and support a large educational bureaucracy. Uncle Abner said no matter what it did for education, the SAD sure gave folks in town plenty of new topics to argue about.

Supporters of the new schools would smile at Uncle Abner's quaint observations, but conclude he was an old-fashioned character from another age and didn't really know what he was talking about.

I thought of Uncle Abner the other day when I read in a newspaper that with two months to go before the year 2000 and its potential Y2K problems, more than a third of the nation's schools and colleges remain unprepared for the new year's potential effect on computers, heating systems and other technology. The report from the U.S. Department of Education said that in the worst of scenarios, some of the nation's schoolchildren could return from Christmas vacation to find heating systems, cafeteria freezers and security systems failing.

Now, when Uncle Abner was responsible for the "heating system" in his island school, they say the system never failed once.

This newspaper article went on to say that the folks in Washington were at odds with local school officials because a survey done by the schools themselves gave an altogether different picture. That survey found that 96 percent of primary and secondary school districts and 97 percent of colleges say they're doing just fine, thank you, and they'll be all set by January 1. On the other hand, the Education Department estimates that 15 percent of the nation's schools will not be ready for the Year 2000 and may have to delay reopening after Christmas vacation.

Who's right? Who knows?

Uncle Abner never knew about computers and such, but he did know that if there was no heat in the school when there was supposed to be, it was his fault. He used to say if you make a school department, or any department, big enough you'll eventually have confusion about who's supposed to be doing what.

Some of these education officials stressed that Y2K-related failures in schools would have little direct impact on teaching and learning, but the failures could—like I said—have an impact on critical operations such as heating and security. They also say teacher paychecks could be held up and student records could be corrupted.

Call me old-fashioned, but I like to think none of this would happen if my Uncle Abner were still in charge of such things.

I read the other day in the newspaper that the Kmart store in Falmouth was closing up shop. Never mind asking what the pioneer of discount stores was doing in upscale Falmouth in the first place, the point is that it's over. Kmart is leaving, closing its doors. It reminded me of the recent headline in a newspaper upcountry that read: "Budget cuts mean new jail may have to close its doors."

Back in the 1960s, when they announced they were building a Kmart in our town, the shopkeepers of the Chamber of Commerce predicted the end of civilization as we had known it in our town. As a teenager, I thought it was all pretty exciting and began wondering what the end of civilization would mean to our town, since it was pretty obvious to me that we could use a little excitement.

Soon after the arrival of Kmart, the phone company announced plans to automate our phone service. The same Chamber of Commerce types who wanted to run Kmart out of town thought the phone changes would lead to a Golden Age in our town. Old-timers began to think the world was coming unglued at the seams.

You might wonder, "What's the connection, John, between your hometown's Kmart and automating the town's phone service, anyway?" The two seemingly unrelated events meant that our little town was changing, and for good or ill, it would never be the same again.

With the new phone system everyone would have to learn and use phone numbers and dial those numbers if they expected their call to go through.

We had never used phone numbers in our town. I was almost fifteen years old at the time and didn't realize that people in our town even had telephone numbers.

In those days the hand-operated switchboard for the town sat in Thelma Ames's cluttered kitchen. She was our town's switchboard operator and she handled every call in and out of town. On rare occasions when Thelma went out, her sis-

ter, Hannah, who lived across the street, would come over to mind the switchboard.

Before automation, you didn't have to know anyone's telephone number. You'd just tell Thelma who you wanted to talk to and she'd connect you.

Thelma didn't need this job. Her family was pretty well off by local standards. The only reason she took the fairly demanding switchboard job was because she wanted to know all the town gossip. And that switchboard job supplied Thelma with a constant supply of raw, unfiltered town gossip.

Like I said before, whenever you wanted to call someone in town you'd pick up the receiver and nosy Thelma would come on and ask who you wanted to talk to. You understood upfront that anything you said on the telephone could, and probably would, be overheard by Thelma Ames.

That kind of eavesdropping may seem like an "invasion of privacy" in our modern, hypersensitive age, but it didn't bother us much, and came in handy on some occasions.

For example, if Mother picked up the phone and asked Thelma to ring Marge Cook over on the river road, Thelma might say something like, "Oh, Alice, I just heard Marge tell Esta Watts that she was going shopping for most of the morning. If you want, I'll give you a ring when Marge gets back." And she would. If you were interested, Thelma could even tell you what Marge said she was going to buy, or what else Marge and Esta talked about.

In this age of e-mail, pagers, answering services, answering machines and cell phones, I'm still not back to the kind of personal service I used to get from Thelma Ames. And Thelma never charged extra.

Since our family had an eight-party line back then, I also figured that there were quite a few other people listening in along with Thelma. I like to think that my public speaking career began with those party line calls of years ago.

And even though I have gone on to speak to larger groups on the radio and in person, I can only hope that my radio audiences listen to me as often, and as intently, as the neighbors back home on that eight-party line.

It takes stories like the Kmart story to remind me that I often miss the old days, and I often agree with those who say, "Not all change has been for the best."

John McDonald

Above all else, John McDonald loves to tell stories about Maine and its people, from Eastport to Kittery and from Fort Kent to Bass Harbor.

To learn more about hiring John for a storytelling event or to learn more about the Maine Storytellers Festival, please visit storytellers.maine.com, or call (207) 743-0757, or email maineauthorjohn.mcdonald@yahoo.com.

John can also be heard Saturday mornings on WGAN 560 AM, read weekly in numerous newspapers throughout the great state of Maine, or found pawing through potential treasures at a yard sale near you.